FINISHED DOG

Charles Jurney

First edition
Manufactured in the United States of America
For information write to:

Charles Jurney
8200 Hwy 150
Terrell, NC 28682

United States copyright office Number Txu 1-011-399

ISBN: 0-9728495-0-5

This book is dedicated to my family for putting up with all the dog mess I have done for the past twenty years. Thanks to the love of my life, Cathy, for going with me and supporting the changes in our lives when I left pharmacy. Thanks to the girls, Alicia and Jessica, for showing me how to use this computer. And to Alicia, for proofing this beast. Thanks to Brian Nicholson for shooting the photos. I love you all. And, thanks to Mark Crawford for putting all this together.

A very special thank you goes to Steve Smith and his best friend, David Meisner. They gave me the opportunity to put things down on paper that went through my mind. They also introduced me to Mr. Gene Hill, the greatest outdoor writer of all time. Gene encouraged me to write a book on the 100 most asked questions of a professional dog trainer. Sorry Gene, I made it to 44 and ran out of gas. The world is a much better place because of Gene Hill and Dave Meisner. They brought so much class.

Lastly, thanks to my Mom and Dad for teaching me some things about honesty, hard work, and being great examples on how to live your life. You have supported me through a lot of crazy things. I love you both more than you will ever know.

CONTENTS:

15. Why does pup need to work on a chain gang?

16. What is an EZ lead and why is it used on dogs?

17. Who was Ivan Petrovich Pavlov and what does he have to do with a dog learning to be obedient?

18. How do you get your dog to wag his tail during force fetching?

19. Do you want to use an electronic collar and have pup like it?

20. How does your dog learn good marking skills and why can't you do it by yourself?

21. What is the best way to make your dog steady without losing desire?

22. How does a dog improve his vision with a marking pattern?

23. How do I begin training pup to handle?

24. What is the easiest way for pup to learn to whistle stop?

25. What is single-T?

26. How do we correct pup's wrong casts?

27. Why do we use double-T?

28.What is the importance of handling on the return?

29.Do you want to use literal or momentum casting?

30.Why does your dog handle well on land but struggle in water?

31.How does your pup learn to take a good initial line?

32.Why do you cast pup around the wagon wheel?

33.Should you run field blinds before mastering the diversion drill?

34.Why will pattern blinds not cause pup problems?

35.What makes pup want to cheat?

36.What does pup learn in a multiple blind drill?

37.Why does pup go to school to learn multiple marks?

38.How can pup learn to honor another dog's work and be happy?

39.Should pup learn to follow his nose?

40.How does pup learn to become a happy upland hunter?

41.Do you want pup to be steady to wing, shot and fall?

42.How do you take pup hunting for the first season?

43.Are these all the skills pup needs to become an event dog?

44.How much pressure is too much?

Foreword

Charlie Jurney is one of those maddening individuals we run across from time to time in life. Maddening because he's what a lot of the rest of us wish we were. In this case, I wish I could train dogs like Charlie can.

Charlie came to dog training in a rather convoluted route that had something to do with pharmacy. I asked him about it one night over a couple of red pops, and he said that he'd been a pharmacist and decided to become a retriever trainer because it seemed like a natural progression. I didn't get the logic of that, but then, as I mentioned, we were having some red pops. Years later, I still don't get it, but it's worked for him.

And it's worked for us amateurs, too. If you want a prescription filled on how to produce a biddable, willing, and non-slip retriever for waterfowl hunting, upland hunting, or field trial/hunt testing, you've come to the right druggist, because Charles Jurney can handle it – and show you how to handle it, too. Charlie has written for a number of top-flight dog magazines, starred in a number of first-class videos (if you see one of these, you'll notice that Charlie is in really good shape and quite handsome – feel free to hate him for that, too, because I do), and is a regular, well-known member of the hunting retriever hunt testing community where his dogs and those he's trained for others excel.

This book takes you from Point A to Point Z and beyond, and the lessons are easy to absorb, digest, and remember. I have seen Charlie's dogs in action and, were he not looking, would have stolen any of them without hesitation.

So I turn you over to Charles Jurney knowing you'll enjoy the journey you're about to make from pup to polished performer – good luck, and have fun.

Steve Smith
Editor
The Retriever Journal
Traverse City, Michigan

CHAPTER ONE

How do we train canines? Learning, Conditioning and Challenging.

What is a finished dog? In my belief, a dog never finishes his training but displays an ability to perform conditioned skills and excellent natural instincts that earn him titles or accolades from retriever organizations. A dog's training begins when his senses awaken in the litter and it continues for life. As a pup, the process is formal and can be confusing but with age he gains maturity and a confidence that allows him to accept any new presentation. Before we can train a dog, we must understand why this species has a desire to learn and how they communicate.

Humans domesticated the canine species thousands of years ago. From the beginning, our race attempted to control the actions of the dogs in any way possible. In the evolution of this process a system of communication skills developed and during the last 50 years, these communication skills between man and dog have reached an all-time high. This is demonstrated every weekend as humans takes canines hunting, field trialing, and hunt testing. In these venues, man and dog work toward common goals and speak a common language.

Communication between humans is most often thought of in a verbal fashion because it is our most proficient method. We use this verbal skill in training our dogs, but truthfully this is the least understood form of communication in a dog's viewpoint. We speak to the dogs with words such as no, *here, heel, sit, kennel, fetch, hold, give, back, over, outside, find it, hunt'em up,* and *good.* These words in themselves carry a great deal of meaning, but the tone in which they are spoken conveys the greatest message to a dog.

Have you ever seen someone that cannot speak to you without using their hands? In recent years, hand gestures and signals have become a well-recognized method of communicating a command to a dog. This is quite an impressive skill when demonstrated by the finished field trial dog running a precise blind retrieve at a great distance. Hand signals are used to cast the dog in a specific direction across fields and ponds to a location that holds a bird. Other trainers use gestures with their hands to instruct their dog to sit, come to them, or stay in a certain position.

Most often, the field trial handler uses a whistle to communicate with his dog. A series of *tweet-tweets* with the whistle may command the dog to return directly to the handler or in Richard Wolters' case, send the dog on a retrieve. When the field trialer blows a single blast on his whistle, the dog immediately sits and awaits his next command. Herding dogs are trained to respond to a multitude of whistle commands at staggering distances while on the run. This is quite an impressive feat and the ultimate in canine/ human communication.

In the early 1960s, Richard Wolters wrote **Water Dog**. In this book, he revolutionized dog training by using a whistle to send the dog on a retrieve. Richard continued his whistle communication with the dogs by calling them to him with a whistle and making them sit at a distance with a whistle. Mr. Wolters called this communication system *whistlese* and in his travels around the world, he educated many of us on the benefits of speaking with a whistle.

Another method to communicate with canines occurs in the way humans carry themselves. This is called postural communication and is closest to the language dogs speak among themselves. An upright body position with the head held up, demonstrates dominance and leadership. On the contrary, a person kneeling with both hands out will welcome a dog to them no matter what their relationship. Raised arms and open hands in a claw like position confer a threatening message to canines and will send them fleeing.

When my wife and I were first married, we lived in a small home. I read the books written by Mr. Wolters and wanted to bring our dogs into the home. However, my bride insisted that the dogs reside in an exterior kennel and therefore, they lived outside. Each morning when I left the house, my dogs would watch me walk out the back door. Some mornings they would stand at the kennel door and beg me to let them out. Other mornings, my best friends would run back into their houses and peek out sheepishly. At first, this made very little sense to me. I began to pay more attention to everything that occurred each morning. It did not take long for me to realize I was the cause of their actions. If I had not slept well the previous night, my dogs ran for their houses. If my wife and I had a relaxing breakfast together, the pups would bark and try to open the kennel doors themselves. In just a few seconds at a distance of 50 yards, my dogs could read my body posture and, know exactly how I felt. That still amazes me to this day.

There is a book of stories about a horse trainer named Monty Roberts that remained on the best sellers list for many months. In this book, Mr. Roberts speaks of a language called Equus. This is the language horses speak while in herds and the way they communicate with each other. When I first read this book, my head began spinning. Monty Roberts was describing actions in horses that I had seen in dogs for many years. While I did recognize that some of the reactions corresponded to certain situations, I did not understand what the pups were trying to tell me. As I spent more time studying his description of the language Equus, the pieces of the puzzle began to fit together in my mind and, the language Canuus became clear.

It is my opinion, the language Equus and the language of dogs, Canuus, are one and the same. Horses and dogs speak different dialects much like those of us in the

South. It is the same language but certain words and phrases in one part of the country have slightly different meanings in another part of the country. My wife became interested in horses years ago and I began to watch their actions and communication. Each day my belief in the language Equus grew stronger, as did the similarities between Equus and Canuus. I see this demonstrated each day as we train in a field adjacent to our horses' pasture. When a dog became confused or received correction, the horses would get as close as they could to the dog. It was not uncommon for them to run across their pasture to check on the dog. In each of these experiences, there was no vocalization on the dog's part. It was communication through body posture and, clearly understood by both species.

While I am comfortable in the belief that the language Canuus exists, I think we as trainers and leaders of dogs need to gain a much greater understanding of the language. It is quite probable that some will read this and scoff at its content demanding their money back before finishing the first chapter. However, there will be others who have a far greater understanding of Canuus than I. They will be the people who truly understand how a dog thinks, communicates and feels during his daily routine. Hopefully in future writings, a greater understanding of Canuus will be available and, our ability to understand what our dogs are saying to us will make us better trainers. Let's take a look at how a dog speaks Canuus.

When most people look at a dog, they focus on his head. So, we will start with head position in an attempt to become fluent in the language Canuus. Think about how many different head positions you have seen your dog assume. When he holds his head upright, much like a snake ready to strike, he is bold and focused. We have two dogs in our kennel that display this posture each time a marked retrieve is presented. Every client that sees these dogs comments about their dramatic posture. The flip side of this presentation is a dog with his head down. Pup is assuming a submissive position and telling everyone that he is no threat. The next time you see a dog with his head down, ask yourself why. Has he received too much pressure or is he worried because he is not sure of his job? Has he just had his tail kicked? Head drop says, "I submit" and, you need to make this feeling in pup disappear.

Avoidance is a very common response from dogs that want to get out of their job. A dog that turns his head to the side and looks away from you is attempting to talk you out of your command. I see this demonstrated many times each day when working with client dogs. Most obedience dogs will turn their heads and look behind me in attempting to avoid my commands. Every dog in the force fetch program at some time will turn his head and look at the back door of our kennel. This response reminds me of an ostrich sticking his head in the sand and saying, “I can't see you, therefore you can't see me. If you can't see me then I do not have to listen to you.”

Attached to a dog’s head are two ears unless we had a training problem before you purchased this book. The position and character of those ears communicates a great deal of what is on pup’s mind. The bold focused dog that we described earlier will always have his ears in an alert position, arched and facing forward. This dog is focused on what is in front of him and is so confident that he has no fear of what might be behind him. He is unafraid and tells the world this by holding his head upright where all can see.

If you have seen many dogs in your life, I am sure that you have seen one with his ears pinned against his head. This guy is worried and fearful of attack. He keeps his ears back in effort to detect any threat that might arise from the rear. I see the laid-back ear position in dogs following corrections during training. Most often, I see this in the pack of dogs that we air each morning. The alpha dogs will correct the beta dogs and the beta dogs will demonstrate this ear position. As soon as the threat passes, the ears come back to a relaxed position and life goes on.

Eye contact is imperative when communicating with any dog. When a dog can see your eyes, he looks into your soul. Now, this can be good or it can be bad. If you have any doubt or fear, pup will see this quickly and, your ability to assume an alpha position will be lost or compromised. However, if you are earnest and committed to be alpha, pup will see that in your eyes. For this reason, I never wear sunglasses when handling or training dogs. I want pup to be able to see into my eyes and know that I mean business.

Quite often when training pressures arise, we see dogs squint. Every time I see this, the dog is telling me that he is anticipating a correction. We have a line of dogs that were bred at our kennel who dramatically demonstrate this eye squint. Jokingly, we have labeled them, Chinese dogs. They are easy dogs to read because they openly communicate with us and because of this, they have become some of our best dogs.

If you are training your dog and he fails to give you eye contact, you have a big problem. Pup is telling you that he does not want to look into your face. It is your job to decide whether he is avoiding you in defiance or, so intimidated that he is afraid to look at you. Avoidance should be corrected in methods we will describe later. Fear should be overcome with affection and loving intonation from you.

One of my clients has a dog named, Ace. His tail is much longer than normal and it has a distinctive curl that acts as a barometer. When high pressure is present, his tail curls up in a tight circle. However, when Ace feels confident and bold his rudder is straight and relaxed. Tail position is a great indicator of confidence and a dog's position in the pecking order. The higher a dog holds his tail, the taller his position on the totem pole. Often we see this while working with our clients. When a client starts to handle their dog, most pups will hold their tails high over their backs. This dog is saying, "I am in control and I am going to lead you." With each passing minute of work, pup's tail starts to drop until it is parallel to his back or even lower. When this occurs, the dog begins to work well and follow the client's lead. At this time, pup has gone from alpha to beta and is willing to accept leadership from the handler.

I am sure you have seen a dog with its tail tucked tightly between its rear legs. This is the ultimate defensive posture and pup is pulling his tail into a position to protect himself. I hope you do not see this response too often, as it means pup is trying to protect himself from you.

Back position is another indicator of how a pup feels. Quite often I see arched backs in dogs that feel uncomfortable. This discomfort can have different sources. It is common for a dog to arch his back after multiple retrieves in cold water. I see this same posture in dogs that have intestinal distress. Arching of the back means distress in some form and the dog needs relief.

Have you ever seen a dog fight? We release from 10 to 20 dogs together each morning before training so they can air themselves. In all of our time, I can only recall a few instances where the dogs became combatants and actually came to blows. Don't get me wrong. I see a great deal of growling, snarling and posturing. Seldom does this position expand into a true fight. One dog will flinch, drop an ear, drop his tail, lower his back, or turn his head away and the fight is over. The alpha dog never flinches. Even in the face of exposed teeth and growling, he holds his ground. From this I learned that in our training, we must never flinch if we are to maintain our alpha position.

Whenever a dog assumes the beta position, he gives the same response every time. That response is a swallow. He may show his tongue or he may keep his mouth closed with a more subtle response. If you gain nothing else from this book, remember the swallow response. When a dog swallows he says, " I understand, I accept and I am no threat to you." I wish this discovery were my own. An animal trainer from Oklahoma named Delmar Smith introduced this concept to me years ago. I did not believe it to be totally true at first. However, I have seen this same response in every dog of every breed since it was first brought to my attention.

The most remarkable thing about a swallow response is that pup does this whether he is accepting praise or correction. That is what confused me when I first started observing this response. How could a dog give you the same action when he was being corrected for misbehavior as when he was being praised for positive actions? It is pup's way of accepting. We are going to talk about acceptance shortly and how important it is for a dog to accept what we present. Knowing when the dog says, "I accept" is the cornerstone of all training and you must be able to recognize it. I have seen a few dogs that give a big sigh along with the swallow response. These guys are shouting instead of whispering, so listen to what they are saying.

When Monty Roberts wrote his book, he made a big deal about the licking and chewing a horse does when he asks to be allowed back into the herd. This response is what made the connection between horses and dogs for me. We had a dog at the kennel named AJ. She was quite insecure and would show a lack of confidence on marked retrieves. On days when I would throw birds for the dogs to retrieve, I learned a great deal from AJ. After she cleared her confidence zone, she began to lick and chew. During her entire hunt she would lick and chew asking her handler if she could return without the bird. AJ eventually developed confidence and became a good marker but she still demonstrates this classic response when she misses her mark.

We have said a great deal about communication and methods of communication to this point. Communication is the basis for all training. We communicate to the pups what we want and they learn what pleases us as well as what angers us. In this communication we ask pup to accept everything we present him. There's a great deal of difference between acceptance and compliance. Acceptance infers willingness to please while compliance refers to force and lack of choice. I had a client at the kennel offer a nice analogy that expresses this in a simple way. In high school compliance occurs because your teachers and parents are present and demand it. Life at college is quite different. Acceptance of routine study habits on your part determined whether you stayed at school or went home and became compliant at a job. A dog that accepts what we present him will be happy and eager to please us. On the other hand, a dog that is forced to be compliant will always look for an opportunity to refuse us and gain his own way.

How do we communicate to the dog what pleases us? There are multiple ways. An upbeat tone in your voice tells pup that you are happy with his work. I prefer to use a soft tone and a stroke on the shoulder. The shoulder stroke is a tool that should be used every time you want to reward the dog for good behavior. When pup was very small his mother would nuzzle him on the shoulder with her muzzle. This is comforting to pup and the most natural reward in the language Canuus. Stroke your dog on the shoulder and watch for the swallow response. When the swallow occurs, stop stroking. Pup is telling you with his swallow that he accepts your thank you and you do not need to continue. Some trainers prosper by using food treats to reward a dog's behavior. I have never recommended this because I feel it creates a dog that is working for himself instead of trying to please you. Stay away from liver treats by telling pup you are happy with his actions through tone of voice and a stroke on the shoulder.

My wife and I have raised two daughters. Many nights when it was time for them to go to bed they would ask for a drink of water, to go to the bathroom or to watch five more minutes of television. This is called displacement behavior. At some time, every dog that I have seen tried to use displacement behavior in an effort to avoid obeying a command. There are five classic responses that demonstrate displacement behavior. Yawning is the first and pup does this not because he is sleepy. He is making an attempt to delay obeying your command. Pups second attempt to evade our control occurs when he scratches at his collar in attempt to remove the collar from his neck. Neck pressure from a leash communicates to pup that he is under the control of someone else. Along with scratching, I see a great number of dogs shaking their heads in hopes of the leash coming off. This is a common method for dogs to remove dirt or water from their coats. In a dog's way of thinking, maybe the leash will come off too. Quite often when walking a dog at heel, pup will drop his head to sniff at the ground. Perhaps this spot is where another dog urinated earlier. His attempt to stop the heeling process by becoming the leader is another example of displacement behavior. When our obedient clients begin working with their dogs, most of the pups will smell and lick at their owner's hands. All of these responses could easily be mistaken for the dog needing to react to an unknown stimulus. In reality, pup is just trying to maintain control of this situation and not forfeit his leadership position. He does this by doing something he wants rather than immediately following our command.

In the beginning of our force fetch program, we have the dogs tethered to a bar above their spine. When clients come in and see these dogs tethered to the bar, the questions begin. Why would you tie the dog up in this position? When faced with pressure all dogs have three responses that are termed "out mechanisms" and the bar takes all three away. The first response is to create space or distance between pup and what is causing him pressure. This is called bolting. In pups mind, the further he is from pressure the less impact or control it has over him. Out response number two is biting. Typically biting occurs when pup cannot bolt. He is in a situation where the pressure is overwhelming and he needs to create the same space or distance as during a bolt. In a bite, pup attempts to bite whatever is causing him pressure thereby, forcing it to bolt from him. The last response to get out of performing a task is to quit. These dogs simply lie down and give up. The dog that lies down in an effort to make pressure go away is most likely a con artist and needs a great deal of extra motivation.

FINISHED DOG

During the training process, a dog learns many conditioned responses. Hopefully, pup will not learn to use displacement behavior and out mechanisms. You might think that all is well when pup accepts your lead and gives up his out responses. However, there are a few more tricks that pup has between his ears. Dogs will perform a skill and challenge you at the same time. These challenges can be very subtle and are often overlooked by most trainers.

When a dog learns to heel, he assumes a position directly beside you. His paw is very close to your foot. Sometimes, it gets a little closer than it should. That is, pup puts his paw directly on top of your foot. I see this happen with every client in their initial training session with their own dog. My blood pressure goes up dramatically when dogs exhibit this challenge. Each time a dog places his foot on an object, in his mind, he is controlling it.

A very similar action from pup that usually follows correction for placing a paw on the trainer's foot is leaning into the trainer's leg. Pup is saying the same thing. If he can lean on you, he is touching you by his own will and therefore, he is in control. The trainer may have commanded pup to assume the heel position. While pup is sitting at heel, he leans into the trainer's leg. The dog is doing what he was commanded to do but is issuing a subtle challenge at the same time. Verbal correction or a little push back is all that is usually needed to correct this misbehavior.

I know quite a few people that are not offended when their dog jumps onto them. This challenge is not subtle. A dog that jumps on you with his paws up on your chest or shoulder is screaming a challenge at you. He is out of your control and on the verge of becoming a demon.

While jumping on you is quite offensive, many trainers often overlook a pup that jumps into you. This usually occurs while pup is returning with a retrieve. He spins to assume the heel position and deliver the bird. While spinning, he slams his body into the trainer's leg. Once again, this dog is telling everyone who is in control and more importantly, that the bird belongs to him.

We see a fair number of dogs bred for the show ring come to our kennel for obedience work. Each of these animals will attempt to carry their leash in their mouth. These guys believe that they control anything they carry in their mouths. In other words, "the leash does not control me, I control it."

Urination and defecation are part of a dog's normal day. It is very important that a dog be given the opportunity to relieve himself before any work begins. By doing this, you are assuring yourself that pup had ample opportunity to empty his bladder and bowels. He should not need to do this while working. Dogs use the ability to put scent on objects as another challenge. If pup relieved himself before you sent him on a retrieve and he repeats the process during the retrieve, he is challenging you. A subtle challenge occurs when he does this in the field at a distance. However, there is nothing subtle about a dog urinating or defecating beside your boot. The dog that attempts to soil the area around you is shouting gross obscenities in your face and needs heavy correction.

Canines communicate in many ways, some are affectionate, some are subtle and others are offensive. Many times I see dogs use a combination of these communication skills in an effort to tell me what they are thinking. The ability to communicate with our dogs is the foundation of our training program. If you cannot communicate your thoughts to a dog and more importantly, understand what he is communicating to you, the success of the training process will be greatly diminished. Start speaking the language Canuus today by paying closer attention to pup's actions and using the language we have described.

Dogs see the world in black and white. I'm not talking about colors, I am referring to the way they view every relationship. Either they are in control or you are in control. There is only one alpha position. As a trainer, you must always assume that position and pup must always be beta. Don't take this wrong, I am not telling you to be heavy-handed or oppressive to your dog while establishing this position. Pup will be perfectly content to accept the beta position if it is presented to him in a comfortable fashion. In every training session you must maintain control of pups actions and control of your thoughts. We will easily control pup's actions with a leash. Control of your thoughts and actions is why I wrote this book and, that may not be quite so easy if you can't speak Canuus.

Training a dog to perform a skill in a reliable fashion involves three steps. The first is learning on the dog's part how to perform the skill. Demonstration of the skill may be required until pup learns what he is supposed to do. This is followed by a conditioning phase that is repetitive and rote. It can be boring for dog and trainer, but it is most necessary. When pup demonstrates a conditioned response, we will go to the final stage of challenging his abilities with every distraction available.

FINISHED DOG

I think it is very important to discuss the duration or length of a training session at this time. Dogs are like children in elementary school. Their attention spans and abilities to focus are short. ***For this reason, we must keep our training sessions short and focused on a goal***. At our kennel, it is common for us to have a training session of less than five minutes if pup met the goals we established prior to the training session. I generally like to limit my training sessions to 10 minutes unless we are in a program such as Double-T that requires more time. The point of emphasis is to watch your dog and understand when pup tells you that he cannot focus any longer.

Something I learned from Monty Roberts was that we do not teach animals. That sounds quite contrary to what you have read or heard in every other training program. I now believe that we do not teach dogs anything, they learn what we are trying to teach them when they are ready to accept. Teaching infers compliance and compliance leads to defiance. Learning speaks of acceptance and willingness to please. So, let's make sure that pup is learning at his own pace and, we are not teaching at our speed. Timetables should never be used when training a dog. They are all individuals and must be trained at a pace that allows them to accept our offerings while being comfortable. During the learning phase, pup must be shown what he is expected to do with ease and comfort on the trainer's part. This will lead to a relaxed pup willing to please his trainer. It builds a strong bond between trainer and dog while making both of them smile.

Step two in the training process involves a tremendous amount of repetition. This leads to a conditioned response much like the response Pavlov saw in his dogs when he rang the dinner bell. In my dealings with amateur trainers, this is always their weak point. Most trainers believe when a dog learns a skill, he understands it and there is no need to repeat that skill. Nothing could be further from the truth, as dogs must be conditioned through repetition to perform precise skills in the face of distractions. Literally thousands of repetitions are required to properly condition a dog. The repetition phase can become extremely boring for both the trainer and dog if you let it be. However, if you mix in a few fun bumpers, a positive tone of voice and a good attitude, both trainer and dog will enjoy the process.

Challenging the conditioned response is the final phase of training. Many things we condition pup to do are contrary to his natural instincts. If we are commanding pup to sit and a cat runs by him, his instincts are going to tell him to chase the cat. This is a big challenge and a test of how well pup accepted his conditioning. Challenges come in many forms; other dogs, cats, people, birds, toys, water, heavy cover, terrain, wind, etc. In tackling a challenge, we present it at a distance initially and gradually move closer as pup's abilities allow. There are formal challenges to test pups abilities. These are called field trials, hunt tests, obedience tests, agility tests, and hunting. In each of these arenas, a dog will be challenged to perform precise skills in the face of great distractions. When a dog and handler are in tune, they become a team and demonstrate the beauty of human/canine communication.

CHAPTER TWO

What is resistance free training?

Can you remember your high school days? Quite often, I have flashbacks to those days and remember the ladies and gentlemen that taught me the courses required for graduation. Some of those memories are quite fond while others are disturbing. Ms. Jennings was one of my English teachers. She required us to stand in front of the class and teach a novel of her choice to the other students. It was a miserable experience and I still cringe when I hear **THE SCARLET LETTER** mentioned. Mrs. Tharpe taught mathematics at our high school. She always made class interesting and challenged us in ways that made us want to work for her. Here was a bunch of high school misfits focusing and trying our best to master the boring skills of mathematics. We resisted Ms. Jennings efforts to teach us because it was not enjoyable. However, we all looked forward to Mrs. Tharpe's smile, which made her subject matter not so boring.

In Mrs. Tharpe's class, we were motivated to work and learn by her enthusiasm and patience. She, like Mary

Poppins, used a little sugar to make the medicine go down. Her sugar was a positive attitude towards her subject and her students. Motivation is a powerful thing. If you find out what motivates me, you can control my life with ease by using that motivation to direct my actions and attitudes. Your job as a trainer of dogs is to find out what motivates your dog and use that motivation to reward and punish your dog. Allowing pup to do what motivates him will be his reward. Taking this away and not satisfying his need to be motivated will be his punishment.

Dogs are part of the small animal kingdom. Before we domesticated them, they lived in the wild with a hole in the ground as their den. They dug the hole large enough to stand up while being able to turn around. When they would go out of the den on a hunt for food, the dogs became vulnerable to the large animals. Lions, tigers and bears were a threat to steal whatever the dogs had captured. The pups were not only in danger of losing a meal for which they had fought hard, but also their lives. For this reason, when dogs captured their game, they returned directly to the den to consume their meal. This chase, capture and return make up the natural instincts all dogs possess to retrieve. Retrieving is one of the most natural instincts all canines have second only to breeding. We want to nurture pup's natural instincts to chase and retrieve by throwing things for him at a very early age. The act of retrieving will be highly motivating to pup when presented to him properly. If we have been good to pup, he should feel secure around us and want to return to us with his catch. His presence near us provides safety and security much like the hole in the ground provided his ancestors. The motivation of retrieving and security at our side are to be nurtured for the rest of pup's life through fun bumpers and, this will be used as a natural reward for good behavior.

When I first heard of resistance free training, it was in the horse journals. I envisioned working the animal without any form of resistance present. As I began to study the subject more, I realized that resistance free training is an attitude and not an action. When we train dogs, it is mandatory that we have a means of controlling the dog's actions. Initially, this is done with a leash. On the surface, this seems contrary to the concept of resistance free training. In earlier discussion we spoke of out responses. Bolting, or attempting to create distance between pup and control (pressure), is overcome with the use of a leash. Pup will learn that he cannot resist or bolt from us when the leash is present and will stop resisting its pressure. Through consistent work and praise pup will learn that we are good and another natural instinct will be nurtured. Every retrieving breed has a natural instinct to please. We want to nurture the desire to please us to such a degree that pup will accept and not resist what we present him.

Resistance free training is not freedom from resistance by the trainer. It is the dog's act of accepting what the trainer presented because he wants to please his trainer. Pup wants to please because he feels comfortable around his trainer and he enjoys what he is being asked to do. This is quite contrary to some of the training programs I was introduced to many years ago. They involved a great deal of force and a lack of focus on what pup thought about the program. The truly finished dog requires no force and is eager to focus on what his handler requests, even in the face of great distractions.

We spoke earlier of leadership and asking pup to accept our lead. Accepting our lead is the essential ingredient in resistance free training. How we ask pup to accept our lead will determine how free from resistance he becomes. If we are rough and heavy-handed, he likely will resist us at every opportunity because he fears us rather than accepts us. But if we are good to pup and, proceed at a pace where he is comfortable, he will be far less likely to resist our presentations. We want pup to speak to us and say, " I accept your leadership role and will not resist you when I am asked to follow your lead."

CHAPTER THREE

Where do we find a dog with the right stuff?

Each time someone calls to ask about locating a puppy, I have flashbacks to my first dog, Sam. I purchased Sam from a friend who had an athletic eager hunting dog. He decided to breed his girl to a very nice looking male whose ancestors found fame in the show ring. I was extremely excited at the thought of bringing home this gorgeous looking puppy and had high hopes of training him to become a perfect hunting dog.

Like many people, I did not take any time to research the breeding and gain some understanding of what this puppy might turn out to be. If the parents were good enough for my friends, then a puppy out of their dogs should be good enough for me. As my knowledge of dogs grew, I realized a mistake had been made in purchasing this puppy. Sam grew up with great looks but little desire to retrieve. He was a mediocre hunting dog and my attempts to train him for hunt tests frustrated both of us greatly. I was attempting to force something into this dog that his genes would not accept. Before you buy a dog, take your time by asking questions of yourself and the seller.

Ask yourself this question first. Do you want a puppy, started dog or finished dog? If you decide to start with a puppy, plan on having a patient training routine and not rushing into a situation that pup is not ready for. Starting with a pup takes dedication on your part but is by far the most rewarding way to go. Some people have a hard time dealing with puppy hood. They look for a started dog to avoid the house breaking, chewing, and other things pups do to annoy their owners. Taking the started dogs forward in training saves you time but there are risks involved. And then, there are the people who need instant gratification. For these folks, you'll occasionally find a finished dog for sale. Which way do you want to go? Let's start with the best way in my opinion, purchasing a puppy.

Before you buy a puppy, a litter must be available. Where you purchase your puppy can have a great deal to do with how successful the training process will be. Getting a puppy from a local neighborhood breeder is a matter of convenience and probably not the best way to locate a future finished dog. I am not telling you to rule out local litters, just be careful when researching your purchase. Pick up any newspaper and the classified advertisements will be full of puppies for sale. Be especially careful of these dogs. Most well bred litters are never advertised because the puppies are sold well before it is time for them to go home. This is the way most professional breeders operate and I recommend that you start your research with a professional breeder. The majority of people who breed puppies professionally spend many hours researching pedigrees and invest years into the type of dog they like. For most of them, this is not a casual hobby but instead, a serious business.

I have never seen a litter that was not promoted as having champion bloodlines. What exactly does this mean? To me, it means the litter owner is forced to sell the merits of his litter because the parents may be something less than finished dogs. If you research every pedigree, you will find a titled dog somewhere in the past. It might be seven generations back, but there still is a champion in these bloodlines. When I look for a puppy, the focus is directed towards the parents and grandparents of the litter. Titled dogs back four or five prior generations mean little or nothing when purchasing a dog.

Champion bloodlines come in many forms depending upon which titles the owners wanted to pursue. When you look at a pedigree, it is common to see many different letters in front of or behind the registered name. What does all this alphabet soup mean? These letters represent titles given by different groups that test or evaluate dogs in their ability to perform certain skills. Don't get excited simply because the dog has a lot of titles in its background. Make sure those titles are in a field similar to what you want your dog to become. CH is a title awarded to dogs on their appearance and conformation. It has nothing to do with the dog's ability to hunt or be trained. I would not recommend you to start training a hunting dog by purchasing a puppy whose pedigree was filled with champion show dogs.

FINISHED DOG

Currently there are several groups that award titles to dogs. NFC, NAFC, FC and AFC titles are awarded to field trial dogs that have earned a certain number of points in particular events. Dogs with these titles have proven that they are capable of being trained to a very high level.

Other pedigrees will have titles such as HR, HRCH, GRHRCH, GMHR, MHR, WR, SR, MH, SH, or JH in front of or behind the registered names. These titles are earned in noncompetitive hunt tests, which emphasize a dog's ability to hunt. Most of this alphabet soup makes the future owner and breeder feel good about what they're doing. In my experience, I have seen many of these titled dogs for which I had little respect. Politics play big a part in the dog world, and quite often dogs do not deserve the titles they receive. So as a buyer beware, just because there are a lot of letters in front of a dog's name, there is no guarantee that the puppies will become finished dogs that their owners will be proud of.

The most reasonable way to locate a well-bred puppy is by doing a great deal of research. Ask each breeder why he bred the parents of the litter. If they cannot document good reasons, you might want to look elsewhere. Any time two dogs are bred, we should strive to improve the breed by matching parents with similar positive traits and dissimilar negative traits. Accentuating positive traits and diminishing negative ones through selective breeding should remove certain faults within a few generations. Before buying a puppy from a breeder, make sure he is doing the right thing by breeding quality dogs for the right reasons.

In looking at past litters, almost every puppy will show striking similarity to either its mother or father in appearance and personality. Ask the litter owner if either of the parents have been bred before. If they have, get names and telephone numbers of the people who purchased previous puppies. Call these folks and see if they are pleased with their purchase. Tell them what your intentions are with your dog and see if they would recommend the breeder to you for that purpose. This is not going to guarantee success but it certainly increases the odds of you getting the type of puppy you desire.

This is a photo of my female, GMHR Lisa's Alligator Alley, with six of her children. All six of these kids qualified at the 1999 RAW NAHRA Invitational in Culpepper, Virginia making the All-American team. This is breeding with the right stuff. Left to Right: HRCH GMHR CJ'S Shortstop, HRCH GMHR Willie Fetch'em Up, GMHR Doc's Little Buddy, GMHR Remington Nitro Express MH, MHR CJ'S Second Blessing, and MHR Megaducks Deal.

FINISHED DOG

My favorite way of finding a puppy that fits my needs involves repeated breedings. I let someone else do the experimenting of seeing what the first litter turned out to be. If the pups out of the first litter look good, have an excellent personality, want to please their owners, show the ability to be trained a high level, have a strong desire to retrieve, and are genetically sound, then I want one out of the next litter. Repeated breedings of good dogs are the safest way for you get a high quality dog.

After you have done your homework and researched quality litters available to you, it is time to hit the road. Look at as many litters as possible so you will not second-guess yourself. It amazes me how many people will purchase a puppy without doing any research. They don't think about the next twelve years that they will be spending with this dog. A word of warning about going to visit prospective litters, ***don't take your checkbook!*** Visiting a litter of puppies can be a highly emotional experience. You may end up buying a dog that does not fit your future needs because you can't tell your children or wife, "No."

FINISHED DOG

Picking the correct litter is the hardest part of buying a puppy. Now it's time to pick the individual puppy that you will be spending a great deal of time with for the next decade. Do you want a little boy or a little girl? I am asked every day whether a male or a female makes a better retriever. I see little difference in the final product. Boys seem to mature quicker but that is not always a good thing. If you can tolerate the female heat cycle, I don't think it matters which gender you choose. However, it can be quite frustrating for your little girl to come into heat the week of a national competition or when you have planned a hunting trip and, your gunning partners all have male dogs. In both cases you and your dog probably don’t get to play.

When it comes time to select your puppy, how does anyone know which pup to choose? I have heard of many tests to evaluate the seven-week-old puppy in hopes of not making a mistake. The problem with these tests is that puppies are rarely consistent in their performances. The most dominant puppy in the litter may be asleep when you show up because he exhausted himself at the food bowl earlier. I prefer to discuss my needs with the breeder and ask him to help me with my puppy selection since he sees the puppies on a more consistent basis. In the final analysis, I let the puppy pick me. If several have caught my eye, I play with them and select the pup that wants to be with me or will not leave my pants leg alone. When unsure, let your wife choose the puppy. We all know that women never make a mistake and therefore will pick the perfect puppy.

FINISHED DOG

But, what if you do not want to deal with puppyhood? Started dogs are sold on a regular basis and can make good gun dogs. The first question that needs to be asked of the seller is, “Why are you selling this dog?” People do not sell good dogs without good reasons, so be sure to get the right answers from the seller before you make your purchase. Most started dogs are sold because the owner has made serious training mistakes or the pup simply does not have what is necessary to become a nice dog. When you are looking at a started dog, there is no way you can begin to evaluate the dog in one or two sessions. Therefore, insist on a 30-day test drive so that you and pup can feel each other out. You may expect this dog to live in the home with you and the seller may have lied to you knowing full well that this pup spent his entire life in a kennel. During this 30-day test drive, try to find as many faults as possible. You'll probably need to visit a professional trainer and enlist his services. A pro can find most dogs’ faults in a short amount of time and save you lots of headaches. If you and pup are compatible and his faults are acceptable, write the seller a check.

If you want a finished dog from a started dog, there is a lot of training to be done. Gain as much information as possible from the seller as to how the dog was trained and what drills it has been conditioned to perform. Revisit the drills so you and pup can get on the same page before moving forward with new material.

Instant gratification has been the American way and that is the choice many people select when looking for a dog. In buying a finished dog, you must be very careful. Few dogs trained to a finished level are sold. This dog will sell for a great deal of money, so make sure he is worth the investment. Find a professional trainer and pay him to drive this dog as hard as possible for a few days. It should not take him long to evaluate the training and potential in the dog.

Each time I hear someone speak of purchasing a finished dog, I chuckle and think of an incident told to me many years ago. A gentleman from the city was told he could purchase a very nice finished dog from a trainer in the next county. So, he hopped in his car and drove out into the country in hopes of purchasing a nice dog and impressing his friends. When he arrived, the trainer was waiting on the dude with his dog trailer. They went out into a field and the trainer took the first prospect out and ran an incredibly difficult blind retrieve with the dog using eleven whistle stops and line corrections. The buyer was mightily impressed and asked the price of the dog. The trainer responded $3000.00. He then went around the trailer and took a dog off to run the same blind. This dog completed the same complex retrieve while only requiring one whistle and line correction. The buyer was so excited that he could hardly contain himself, "How much for that dog?" The trainer dropped his head and explained this was his personal dog but times were hard. He only offered this dog for sale because he needed money to pay for his son's operation. The trainer said, "I can't take anything less than $5000.00 for my dog." The city slicker quickly took the cash out and paid the trainer. Feeling like he had stolen a nice dog at a bargain price, he then headed back to town. The trainer returned to his farm and was met by his wife who asked how things had gone. Which dog did the man buy? The trainer replied that he had only taken one dog and ran the same blind retrieve twice with the same dog. Of course the dog ran it much better on the second try because he knew where to go. The gentleman from town was so excited that he did not pay attention to what was happening. The trainer and his wife had a great laugh while they planned their vacation to the Hawaii. Be careful with trainers and the dogs they run, things may not be as they appear.

CHAPTER FOUR

What is the most traumatic time in pup's life?

Have you ever been homesick? My stomach churns each time I think about Elks Camp For Boys in the mountains of North Carolina. I attended this camp for a couple of summers and had a wonderful experience on those trips. But, my third trip to the mountains found me insecure and wanting to return home. I wrote my parents letters asking them to please come get me. They could not resist their youngest son and drove to the mountains to pick me up. I'm sure many of you have had similar experiences with being home sick. It is a miserable feeling.

Just as I had to leave my parents and go to camp, a pup must leave his mother and litter mates. This is a terribly traumatic time for pup and a most important time for us to develop a leadership and maternal role with our future champion. When leaving the litter, a puppy loses everything in his life that was secure and safe. He no longer has his mother to watch over him and provide a secure place to sleep. A pup also loses his security when leaving his siblings because in the litter pecking order, he knew his place and was comfortable with that position. Imagine yourself being taken from your family to a foreign land where you understood nothing that was being spoken. It would be nice to have someone looking over your shoulder, providing shelter, food and attention. In a short period of time, you and this person would likely form a very close relationship because this person was good to you and made you feel comfortable.

During a puppy's first six weeks, he learns everything from his mother. And much like my mother, a pup's mother never lies to him or places him in a position of danger. If you decide to purchase a puppy, it is your responsibility to take the maternal role in the puppy's life. He will look to you for guidance and security whenever something new is presented. This is a tremendous responsibility and must be taken seriously. You have the opportunity to form a personality that will dedicate its life to you forever.

In a puppy's first days away from its mother, it will search for something with which to form a bond. This bond will be life-long and according to researchers is the strongest bond ever to be formed in that animal's life. I have been amazed many times when working with clients and their dogs at how strong this bond actually can become. Grayson Chesser brought his dog, Bubba, to my kennel many years ago for training. Bubba stayed at the kennel in training for around eight months and he became a very well trained dog. He could run complex triples, difficult blinds at any distance and would have been comfortable shopping with me in the grocery store. Grayson was coming to pick Bubba up and wanted to know where I would be training that day. I gave him directions to our location but decided at the last minute to change my specific location in the field. I saw Grayson pull into the wrong to end of the field and took Bubba off my truck at that time. Bubba looked up and saw Grayson standing some 400 yards away. He was so excited to see his owner that he bolted to Grayson totally out of control. My best efforts could not stop Bubba from going to see his best friend, Grayson. His bond with his owner was far greater than the training skills I had conditioned into Bubba. I tell this story to all of my clients who worry about their dogs forgetting them while in training. Dogs never forget who became their foster mother when they left their actual mother. This is an important time in your dog's life and you can form a very special bond if you take the time to satisfy your puppy's needs.

The bond we have discussed so far is not always formed with people. Leaving two littermates together for an extended period is not a good idea. Each time I've seen this happen, the puppies bonded with each other and they looked to each other for security. These guys are not easy to train because they do not totally trust us. The bond formation can also occur with inanimate objects. I can think of at least ten dogs that have come to me for training that had formed a previous bond with their water buckets. This is a scary dog. He prefers to spend time chasing and carrying a metal bucket around his kennel instead of playing with us and chasing birds. Invariably, these pups were placed in an outdoor kennel when they came home from the litter and had very little human contact each day. Please, make sure your puppy never prefers to chase his water bucket instead of spending time with you.

At our training facility, we work with approximately 40 dogs each day. It is amazing what some of these dogs will tell you in their actions and postures speaking the language Canuus. Our staff will congratulate a client that has spent a great deal of time with their dog before bringing him to the kennel. It becomes very evident to us who has and has not spent time with their puppy and socialized them. This is emphasized when the clients come for their initial visits in how the dogs react while wanting to please their owners.

So, if you're going to purchase a puppy from a litter, a great opportunity lies ahead of you. Now is the time to form that life-long bond necessary if you want your dog to go on and become a finished dog. Failing to take advantage of pup's vulnerability at this critical time in his life can cause staggering social problems that will lead to an inability to accept training. Playing with a puppy is one of the most enjoyable facets of my job. If you cannot spend time with your puppy and form a strong bond through daily contact, you probably do not deserve to own a dog and should take up some other activity.

CHAPTER FIVE

Why are the first six months the most important time in a puppy's life?

In his writings, Richard Wolters continually emphasized the learning phases a puppy goes through during his first six months. In this period, his brain goes from nonfunctional to completely formed and ready to accept any information provided by the outside world. It is important on our part to make sure the right information goes into pup's brain and not rely on him to be both student and teacher. Initial introduction to everything that will be important in the dog's life should be done in a comfortable and relaxed manner before pup reaches the age of six months. This does not mean he should be a finished retriever at six months of age, but rather that he should not be afraid of anything new.

FINISHED DOG

As a newborn puppy, he relies upon his mother for food, shelter, love and discipline. She will be his first disciplinarian and he will learn to accept correction from Mama in a comfortable fashion. We seldom give these initial caretakers enough credit for the job they do in preparing their children for us to train. She sets the table and makes it easy for us to step in and take her place by disciplining a rowdy pup at one minute and caressing him softly at another. These grand dams give each puppy detailed instruction in the language Canuus well before the age of seven weeks.

In the litter a very strong and distinctive pecking order is formed. Each puppy learns how to accept correction from siblings as betas and how to be tough guys as alphas. The alpha-beta relationship begins with Mama and is greatly expanded each passing day as the litter approaches seven weeks of age. They fight for food by pushing each other out of the food bowl and wrestle with each other's ears until submission occurs. If you sit back and think about this, a puppy has already learned how their world works before we ever take them home to our world.

Trauma and recovery from trauma are quickly learned and accepted by the puppies when we steal them from their mothers at seven weeks of age. A strong secure bond is rapidly formed at this time, which allows us to develop a "want to please attitude" in the puppy. The stage is quickly being set for our training program, so make good use of it.

From this time forward, we will introduce many objects, smells, sounds, touches, and places. How they are introduced and accepted by pup will determine how successful the training process will be and whether we are going to develop a finished dog. You get one chance to do this right much like your first impression with each person you meet in your life. Done properly, pup's first impression of all new subjects will be good and make learning fun. Speeding up the training program to your pace and skipping subject matter will lead to a bad attitude towards training and holes in the program. Or you can just do nothing and let pup learn what he wants to. Good, bad or indifferent, it is your choice. Now is the time to introduce your pup to the world according to you and your needs for your finished dog.

FINISHED DOG

CHAPTER SIX

Why is crate training a good thing?

Socializing your new puppy to a crate is extremely critical. Some people see a puppy in a crate and think of how cruel it is to leave the pup in the crate. Nothing can be further from the truth. In most cases, people who complain about dogs in crates place themselves in the dog's position and do not think about what is best for the dog. Generally, these people do not think like a dog and therefore cannot understand why the dog would enjoy being in a crate.

When dogs lived in the wild prior to domestication, their home was a hole in the ground. This den was big enough to turn around and stand up in. It provided protection and security from the world around them. Earlier we discussed the area around us becoming a sanctuary for pup. It is now time to transfer that security to the crate.

FINISHED DOG

If we're going to properly socialize our puppy, it is imperative that he be able to travel with us and enjoy the daily life experiences that will make him a well-rounded dog. Traveling without pup in a crate can become a life-threatening experience for our best friend. I have a veterinarian for a client that was recently involved in a head-on collision. Both of his dogs were riding in the front seat with him. His Labrador Retriever was uninjured in the crash but his Jack Russell Terrier suffered a fractured pelvis. This could have been prevented had the dogs been secured in their crates. The vet was slightly injured being stunned by the collision and lost his focus on the dogs. Thank goodness, people stopped to assist the victims of the wreck preventing the dogs from running through traffic and probably being killed.

So, socialize your puppy to a crate and take him everywhere you go. If he can travel in a crate comfortably, necessary trips to the veterinarian will be a walk in the park. A hunting trip to Canada that requires traveling on an airplane will be much less stressful if your dog is comfortable in his crate. Your little girl may become one of the best field trial dogs in the country. If you have selected a boyfriend for her that resides six states away, shipping her by air to her beau will not be a difficult experience as long as she feels secure in her crate. Family vacations should include your dog and taking him with you becomes quite easy after crate training. Each of these situations demonstrates the need for your dog to feel relaxed and at ease while in a crate.

How big should your crate be? I see many people buy the largest crate available thinking this will make their dog happy. The idea of bigger being better does not relate to purchasing crates. For the puppy, you should purchase a puppy crate just large enough for him to stand up in and turn around. House breaking is just around corner and a small crate will make this job easier. As your dog grows, a larger crate needs to be purchased. Whatever size crate you decide upon, make sure it has the ability to be cleaned without much trouble.

Now that you have purchased a crate, how do we get our puppy to go into this thing. Initially, pup will probably fight your insisting him to enter the crate. He is enjoying life with you and does not want to be separated from his foster mother. This is a good thing. However, he needs to understand that his crate will cause him no harm and will provide security when you are not present. At first, I will pick up pup and place him inside the kennel while saying, "Kennel." Normally pup will turn around and run out of the kennel. Repeat the process a few times, finally closing the door behind him.

But what if you purchased a started dog that has not been properly socialized to a crate? How do we get this guy into the crate without going in there with him? Attach a leash to his collar running the end of the leash through an opening in the back wall of the kennel. Using leash pressure, pull your dog into the kennel while commanding, "Kennel." This needs to be repeated many times until the proper conditioned response follows your command.

When all else fails, place your dog's food bowl in the crate and feed him there each night. Seldom is this necessary, but it can be used as a method of getting your dog into the kennel without force if he is anxious about the situation. After he becomes comfortable in the kennel, go back to the previous methods we have discussed to thoroughly condition the "Kennel" command.

I have never placed a dog in a crate that did not immediately begin screaming his lungs out. "Daddy, please come get me!" is shouted by the puppy until exhaustion occurs or, we give in. When I operated a pharmacy, it was not uncommon to hear a screaming puppy crated in the back room. This was my method of allowing pup to accept his situation and not gain anything by barking. My rule was that pup could not exit the kennel until he stopped barking. Now is the time to decide if you want your pup to become a barking nuisance or a good citizen. Checking on your pup or taking him out of the crate while he is barking rewards his noisy behavior with your presence. Just like the crying baby, let him lie. Eventually, he will learn that the only thing he gets for barking is tired. A dog barking in his crate at 2a.m. will test your patience, so be steadfast.

House breaking can be done in short order when your dog is comfortable in a crate. If puppy likes his crate, he is unlikely to soil the nesting area. We can use this to our advantage when conditioning pup to relieve himself. None of us kept our diapers clean when we were babies, so don't expect your pup to be perfect in his house breaking. I have seen this process take from two days to three months. As with children, pup will dictate the pace at which we proceed.

The rules for house training involve five situations where pup must go outside and do his business before he can return to the home. On each visit to the yard, we hurry to the same spot. This becomes a magic spot because pup can visually see where he has been. Also, his nose will tell him what he did there previously and this will stimulate him to go again. While pup is in the act of doing his business, we need to add a command. I have heard many different commands ranging from silly to hilarious, but I like to use the command, “Outside”. Through repetition and conditioning, your dog will squat on command.

The first situation, which requires pup to go outside and do his business, is when he exits his crate. It does not matter if the relieved himself a few minutes earlier, pup still must go outside and cannot come back into the house until he has attempted to relieve himself. This is not a lot of fun when it is pouring down rain and 33 degrees, but it is necessary for proper training.

Each time a puppy eats or drinks, he goes outside. His digestive tract will be stimulated and if you do not get him outside shortly, you will probably find a prize behind your favorite chair.

Puppies sleep a great deal while in the crates. This is a sign that they are content and relaxed. Following each nap, pup needs to visit his magic spot in the yard and relieve himself before going on to another activity.

I love to play with puppies in the house. This is a great socialization time for pup and makes me feel good. It is easy to lose track of time during these play sessions and that can lead to accidents by pup around the home. If your puppy has been playing in the house for more than one hour, it's time to go outside and find the magic spot. Imagine how easy taking pup on trips will be when you don't have to spend a great deal of time waiting on him to relieve himself because you have conditioned this through daily training.

Here’s one final thought on crate training. Let's pretend the Internal Revenue Service has an appointment at your home tomorrow afternoon. An agent knocks at your door and states, “ I hate dogs!” when he sees your pup. Aren’t you happy your dog can be quiet and content in a crate out of sight?

CHAPTER SEVEN

Should you keep your dog in the home or in a kennel?

Richard Wolters came along with some extremely radical ideas in early 1960s. None of them was more controversial than his suggestion that retrievers should be kept in the home rather than in a backyard kennel. The status quo at that time believed that keeping the dog in home would ruin the dog's ability to smell and dampen their desire to hunt. Richard developed a number of other ideas that were equally radical from training with a whistle to starting the training process at seven weeks of age. However, in my mind, Mr. Wolters' greatest contribution to retrievers was showing us that their proper place was in the home beside us.

We spoke earlier of communication in a nonverbal fashion. Living with your retriever 24 hours a day is akin to sharing a dormitory room with a foreign exchange student. In a short period of time, both of you will learn how to speak the other one's language. Now that you have an understanding of the language Canuus, you and pup should be able to converse openly in your home. Pup will also learn what each tone in your voice means as you communicate with other members in the family. His ability to read your eyes and posture will grow exponentially. With time, you will be able to read pup's posture and determine when he is uncomfortable with something new or happy to oblige your request. My bride is great at evaluating attitudes of all species of animals simply by watching them for a few minutes. She developed this is as child by adopting and nurturing many different animals. Daily contact with these orphans has made her into a modern day Dr. Doolittle. These are examples of improved communication skills that can be developed by constant contact with your pup if you will simply spend more time with him by allowing him to share your living space.

In your home, there are many areas, which will invite pup to explore and learn. Each of these areas will present a different set of hazards and with these hazards, comes a great training opportunity. If your dog is kept in an outdoor kennel, the only time you can train him is when he is taken from the kennel. Think of your daily routine and all the training opportunities you would have if your puppy lived in the home with you. Taking out the garbage could easily incorporate a heeling drill. Pup could learn to remain seated for an extended period of time while you are having supper or working at your desk. Retrieving can be nurtured in a hallway. Think of the possibilities and never miss an opportunity to train. Most importantly, the word “NO” will take on far greater meaning because pup will hear this each time he strays into a wrong area or action. It will not take pup long to learn the varying tones of your voice when you use the word "NO" and with this, you are developing the communication skills that will make you fluent in Canuus.

Many retriever owners fail to spend time with their dog except when training. In the home, you and pup will spend many more hours together than if he were outside. With this time comes a stronger bond between you and pup. Nothing can be more important in your training program than developing a watertight bond, which will lead to a strong desire to please by pup. All future training will result from this bond and desire to please you. We are trying to develop a dog that is secure and comfortable in our presence. If we do this by constantly communicating with our puppy in the home, he will rapidly accept all of our training offerings and the puzzle of training will become much easier for you.

Your home is probably like mine, in that you have a few prized possessions lying around. Your house can become a minefield to pup because he will most likely hear the word "NO" screamed at him each time he nears one of the valuables. Suppose your Aunt Edna left you an antique chair worth thousands of dollars and your puppy decides to ease his teething pain on one of the legs. His life in the home will probably be short when your wife finds out. So, when you have an object that means more to you than your pup, get it up out of harm's way. He is going to investigate the world. This is done by putting things in his mouth much like we did what we were infant children. He learns how things feel and the weight of different objects. Few of us would leave a toddler free to run around our home and play with valuable possessions, so why should pup be any different?

Myths are quite popular when it comes to training a dog. I never have understood why people want to believe some of these outlandish offerings. Not having your hunting dog in the home has been at the top of the list for training myths. In all of my readings and studying of dogs, I have yet to find one piece of evidence supporting the theory that a dog loses any olfactory capabilities due to living in the home. Likewise, no one has shown me why a dog that sleeps by your bed is less inclined to become an excellent hunter in the duck blind. Contrary to a popular belief from decades ago, your dog can be a good pet and a good hunter at the same time while having the same mailing address as you.

Let suppose for argument's sake that you want to keep your dog in an outdoor kennel. What's the harm? First of all, he is out of sight and therefore, out of mind. If you don't have a strong bond with your puppy, I guess this is okay. It can be a convenient arrangement unless it's pouring down rain at feeding time. And then there are the runs to clean and, that wonderful smell that surrounds the dog kennel. Bowls must be washed and carried outside each day at feeding time. If you live in a neighborhood association, I'm sure no one will mind that eyesore in your backyard. In just a short period of time, pup will likely form the strongest bond of his life with a food bowl or water bucket. He will lack for attention and beg for you to rescue him from this predicament with constant barking. Does this sound like a good way to form a strong bond between you and your best friend? I don't think so. Get your pup in the home with you and keep him there!

FINISHED DOG

CHAPTER EIGHT

When do you introduce your pup to a collar and leash?

Controlling pup in each training session is mandatory if we want our training program to proceed in an orderly fashion. Our initial training control comes through the use of a leash, which is attached to a collar around pup's neck. Having a collar placed around a dog's neck can be an uncomfortable and worrisome process for almost every dog. Acceptance of the collar and leash is necessary before we can go along to any further training, so let's cross this bridge as soon as possible.

When you go to pick your dog up, whether it is a puppy, started dog or finish dog, you need to take a proper fitting collar with you. This collar should be placed around the pup's neck immediately. He will gradually become comfortable while wearing the collar if the socialization is allowed to occur at his pace. By this, I mean he needs to be relaxed and not worrying about the collar around his neck. He should not be scratching, clawing or trying to back out of the collar. Normally, a puppy will scratch at his collar in an attempt to remove it from his neck. He will use his feet in an effort to push the collar over his head or get it in his mouth. In both cases pup is trying to control the collar because as you remember from our previous discussion, anything pup can put his paw or mouth on, he is controlling. So, when the scratching stops it is time to attach a leash to the collar.

As with a collar, our future star needs to learn to accept the attachment of a leash to his collar and be comfortable with this situation. While this sounds quite simple, I have seen many dogs over the years fail to accept the fact that a leash would be attached to their collar. Initially when I attach a leash, pup will be in the yard free to run without any restraint from the leash. If things are going well, he will run around the yard dragging the leash behind him and, in short order forget that it is attached. Once this is accomplished, it is nice to have another dog that likes to chase and catch the leash. In doing this, the other dog is placing pup in the position to learn what leash restraint means. In pup's mind we are not associated with that pull around his neck and the control that goes along with each tug. Soon, pup will learn not to fight the pressure of a leash and at that, time we will begin to pick up the leash ourselves.

Now it's time to begin a very serious lesson. Pup’s leash must represent total control to him. He will try to pull and back out of the leash initially and this must not be allowed. If through a mistake on our part, pup learns that pulling on his leash will gain him freedom from our control, we have set a very bad training precedent. Most young dogs will pull in every direction. If freedom does not come, they will plop down and give up. When you see this occur as you're walking your puppy, it is time to begin tying him to various objects with the leash. I like to begin this initial stake out work by tethering pup in to a doorknob in the house. Just like crate training, his barking is not to be rewarded by our presence or recognition. From the doorknob in the house we need to proceed to a tree in the yard. Find anything in your training areas and attach pup to it by his leash until he accepts this situation in a calm and relaxed manner. While this first step seems small, it is a giant leap in pup's mind. He is accepting control from the leash through a collar and is learning to be steered by this pressure. Do not be in a hurry to speed this process up. Until he accepts his situation, we cannot proceed to the next step.

We have not talked about what type of collar to use. I prefer nylon collars with metal buckles. For many years I used collars with plastic snaps. This brand proved to be inefficient when trying to control the actions of a non-socialized, one hundred pound, out of control dog. Leather collars also work well if the thickness is sufficient to prevent breaking.

New clients at our kennel are constantly questioning me as to why the collar around their dog's neck is so tight. I explain that if the collar can slide over the dog's head, it serves no purpose. If I can comfortably get two fingers between the collar and the dog's neck, it should function properly by staying in the correct position and not slide over pup's head. Correct collar position is debated often but is very clear in my mind. Collars should not be hanging around the dog's neck just above the shoulders. In this position, the collar acts as a harness and promotes pulling by the dog. All dogs have a sledding mentality and can pull against shoulder pressure indefinitely. Therefore, make sure the collar is snugly positioned directly behind pup's ears. As with us, dogs have pressure points directly behind their ears and we need our collar to work on these points if we are to control pup's actions.

Now that we have the collar squared away, let's discuss our leash. For initial puppy work, I like to use a quarter inch nylon rope approximately six feet long. No knots are to be tied in the end of the leash so it can slip and slide around our home without snagging on a table leg and causing the contents of the table to spill. Later in training, we will add whatever length rope is necessary to control pup's actions. A few chapters ahead in this book, we will introduce you to a special training leash that will make your life and pup's much more enjoyable. A word of warning, stay away from the retractable leash that is so popular in most pet stores until pup's obedience training is finished. This type of leash gives a dog some latitude by pushing a button and extending the length of the leash. While it sounds nice, your dog will quickly learn that pulling on a leash will give him more freedom. This is the opposite of what we are trying to accomplish so stick with a plain Jane rope leash.

CHAPTER NINE

What are fun bumpers and how do we use them?

In previous chapters we have discussed a dog's natural instinct to retrieve. This driving desire to chase and retrieve is secondary only to the desire to reproduce. What makes this chase and retrieve so motivating to our dogs? It was the fashion in which they gained sustenance by chasing small game and then retrieving it to their den for consumption. How many of us are not motivated by a nice meal?

Now that we understand why dogs are motivated to retrieve, let's discuss how to use retrieving as an attitude adjuster. Fun bumpers are thrown for dogs to nurture desire to retrieve when they are young puppies. Later in life, they are used to change pup's outlook on uncomfortable situations. With the young puppy, we are constantly throwing objects for him to retrieve in an effort to start the mechanics of retrieving to our side. Very few puppies of any breed will not chase objects and retrieve them if this game is started early in the dog's life. The action of chasing and retrieving rewards pup in a natural fashion. If we continue playing a chase and retrieve game throughout pup's adolescence, it will also become a great motivator.

In most of our training sessions, we have set rules that pup is required to follow. The only rule in the game of fun bumpers is that pup must chase the bumper. He is not required to retrieve it or remain seated before it is thrown. If our future star decides to pick up the bumper and return to us with it, this is a bonus but not a requirement. Later in his life following the force fetch process he will be required to deliver each bumper to our side. During the initial introduction of fun bumpers it is desirable for pup to carry the bumper around in his mouth. For this reason, you should not take a bumper from pup's mouth when he returns to you. I prefer to let the puppy drop the bumper on his own before I tease him and throw it again. In a pup's mind, he has worked hard for his prize and wants to keep it for himself. If we try to take it from his mouth, he thinks we are stealing his prize and this will lead to him running from us instead of returning to our side.

Questions are quite often asked of professional trainers concerning dogs that have a poor desire to retrieve. How do I get my dog to retrieve and be happy about it? What should I do if my puppy fails to chase a fun bumper? In both cases, teasing the dog with a bumper or bird until he becomes excited is the answer. It serves no purpose to throw an object for our dogs to retrieve if they're not motivated. Motivation can be nurtured in the teasing process by taunting your dog with a bird or bumper until he becomes excited. As pup's interest in the object intensifies, toss it a few feet in front of him. If the chase does not occur continue to tease pup with the object and repeat the process. I've seen this go on for days and weeks in an unmotivated student. Patience on the trainer's part is the only way to solve this problem. I've yet to see a dog enjoy retrieving that had this process forced upon him. So, start the fun bumper program as an exciting game and continue it throughout pup's life.

Later in pup's training, we're going to demand him to remain steady until he is sent to retrieve. Therefore, it is imperative that we add a verbal command to differentiate the fun bumper routine. I use the words, "Hup, Hup, Hup" prior to tossing the fun bumper as a verbal cue to pup that we are about to have fun chasing a bumper. You can use any words you prefer but you should be consistent so that the same message is communicated to pup each time. In short order, the verbal cue alone will send your pup into a frenzy of excitement and enthusiasm.

Wouldn't it be nice in our daily routines if someone could stop by and say a few words to us that would make all of our cares go away? Life would be a dream if our negative attitudes could be adjusted to a point where we would be laughing and happy with only the saying of a few words. That is exactly the purpose and function of fun bumpers. In my opinion, this is the most important skill ever learned by a retriever.

How and when do we use fun bumpers? I throw fun bumpers everyday during the training of each dog in some form or fashion. Each training session with a young dog begins by tossing a few fun bumpers. This is continued until I can see a positive attitude in the pup. I believe any student possessing a positive attitude will be far more likely to learn what we are presenting and happy to please us. Isn't that exactly what we're trying to accomplish in every training session?

Continual repetition will condition a very positive response to your verbal cue and pup will always seek his fun bumper when he hears the magic words. With this comes the ability to overcome new situations that might seem dangerous or worrisome to pup. Simply tossing a few fun bumpers into or around the hazard will quickly change pup's attitude toward the problem. We use this quite often at our kennel when coaxing a dog into the water for the first time. It is also my tool of choice for pup's initial entrance into heavy cover or across roadways. Most dogs become confused and unconfident during the initial training sessions of double-T and swim-by. I insist on adjusting pup's attitude with a few fun bumpers every time confusion or a lack of confidence appears.

Fun bumpers are enjoyable for us just as they are for the dogs. I do not know anyone who does not smile when their dog retrieves with a wagging tail and happy attitude. For this reason, I see a lot of people who throw far too many fun bumpers for their dogs. The positive effect of fun bumpers is lost by throwing too many. It is kind of like eating prime rib for lunch everyday. After a while, it no longer tastes good. So, it is good to keep the number of retrieves small. While I am not going to give you an exact number, I seldom throw more than two or three fun bumpers at a time. Your main focus needs to be on pup's attitude. Throw fun bumpers until you see the *tail wag the dog.*

Fun bumpers will later be used to reward and punish pup for according behavior. One or two fun bumpers will always follow the job well done before putting pup back on the truck. By doing this, we will only increase his desire to work for us in our next training session. Starting the next training session off with a few fun bumpers will quickly put pup in a frame of mine to please us and learn what we are presenting.

How do we punish a dog with fun bumpers? Most of us like to make money and we are rewarded in our daily jobs with a paycheck each week. Suppose your boss told you that your paycheck depended on how well you performed your job. You do a good job and he will give you a big paycheck. You do a poor job and there will be no paycheck for you. Motivation is a strong tool and the motivation to receive your paycheck for a job well done keeps you at work. Poor performances by pup in his work or lack of desire to please us will find him put away without his paycheck of fun bumpers. Not giving a dog his fun bumper can be the greatest punishment in a dog's life if he has been properly trained with them.

The rest of this book is dedicated to the learning of specific drills that lead to a finished dog. These drills are like tools in a carpenter's toolbox. You will have the ability to look in your toolbox and pull out a drill that can fix any training problem. Fun bumpers are the first and foremost tool in the box.

CHAPTER TEN

Do you want your dog to retrieve decoys?

I have a friend who owns a dog named, Dan. Daniel is an extremely well trained dog and will retrieve virtually anything when asked to do so. It is not uncommon for Dan to carry a bumper out and plant it as a blind for another dog in his training group. It is also not uncommon for him to retrieve the entire decoy rig following a hunt. The key to this is that Dan performs this skill on command. I can see a lot of you sitting in your chairs reading this and wondering how to teach your dog to pick up all of your decoys so you will no have to. That is not the purpose of this chapter. While it is quite intriguing and a great stunt to show your hunting buddies, it can also get you in trouble.

I have another friend with a dog named, Willie. Young William has quite an attitude and will look for a way out of a problem instead of trying to please his owner by accepting what is asked. During the middle of last duck season, I received a phone call from Willie's owner. He was at a high-class hunting lodge on the coast of North Carolina sharing a blind with a group of very influential people. They were having a successful hunt and Willie was doing a respectable job of bringing the chickens home. During the hunt, a bird drifted outside the decoy rig and young William was asked to run a blind retrieve. The water was cold and choppy. Willie decided to retrieve a decoy in hopes of satisfying his owner and getting back to the boat as quickly as possible. This was not a good decision as his owner forced him back into the water and out to the bird with the aid of an electronic collar. Young William placed a lot of egg on his owner's face during this escapade and fueled many jokes at the supper table that evening. I hope you have higher expectations from your dog than retrieving decoys.

Decoy introduction needs to occur when a pup is young and not likely to be intimidated by the blocks and their lines. As a rule, we keep decoys in the yard at our training kennel. The dogs see them everyday and quickly lose interest in them. This is passive introduction because the dogs run around the decoys each day while working on other skills. Occasionally, one of our dogs will show an active interest in the decoys. This pup needs a formal introduction program to insure that he will keep his owner off the receiving end of many jokes.

FINISHED DOG

The formal program starts with about a dozen decoys spread throughout the yard. Place your dog on a leash and walk him around the outer edge of the decoys. Pay attention to his attitude. As he relaxes, direct your walk into the decoy rig at a slow pace. Walk around all of the decoys, allowing pup to smell and investigate each of these odd creatures. He is allowed to smell them but should be scolded if he tries to pick them up or place a paw on them. Repeat this process until he is totally relaxed while walking through the rig. This may take five minutes or five days, pup will tell us how long.

Now it is time for your dog to learn how to retrieve in the presence of decoys. Before you can do this, he must be happily retrieving fun bumpers in the area were you have placed the decoys. Initially, toss a few fun bumpers beside the decoy rig. Pour the praise on with each enthusiastic retrieve, letting pup know you are happy with his actions. Gradually move the location of the bumper to the opposite side of the decoys so that pup is required to run through the entire rig when making the retrieve. If he decides to run around the decoys instead of through them, position yourself among the decoys to receive the bumper. Repeat this until he will run through the decoys without hesitation and return directly to you through the decoys.

Next, you need to throw the fun bumpers into the middle of the decoy spread. This should go well unless you had problems with the last step. Once again, repetition is the key to desensitizing your dog to decoys. If he should try to pick one up or stop and smell any of the blocks, quickly enter the decoy rig yourself and tease pup with the bumper until it has his entire interest. Continue throwing fun bumpers in this environment until your puppy sees nothing but the bumper. After his comfortable with feathers, you need to repeat this process with a bird.

At this point, your dog should have no worries about decoys. Now is the time to move your decoy rig from land to water. An ideal piece of water would be shallow enough to be waded, in case you need to walk out into the water with pup and reassure him. Start by throwing a few fun bumpers beside the decoys. When he relaxes with this situation, move your tosses beyond the decoy rig and then into the decoys just as you did on land. It is not uncommon for a dog to be worried or frightened by a decoy when he bumps into one. Let him know the plastic birds will not harm him by rewarding each of his retrieves with enthusiasm. Decoy lines should be short so pup will not become entangled in them.

Decoys should become a regular part of your training program. Your training fields and ponds need to have decoys in them each day you go out to work. While some of this may seem to be overkill, do you want to take a chance that your dog will become decoy shy? I don't think so. You will not look very good with egg on your face.

CHAPTER ELEVEN

Why do some dogs not like going into the water?

Have you ever seen a dog that was afraid to retrieve in water? I have many times and it makes me sick. Quite often, people bring us dogs for training from six months to three years in age. It is not uncommon for these dogs to have never seen water other than in their food bowl. Our initial work with them is uncomfortable for all parties and this situation is inexcusable for the owner.

Champ came to our kennel when he was about eight months old. His breeding was not outstanding but it was certainly good enough to produce a respectable gun dog. In working with him around the water, it was quite clear that he hated the thought of swimming. Champ's attitude told us that he had a bad experience in or around water at some point in his life. The client was questioned and later, the beans were spilled. Champ had refused to retrieve in water for the client, so he was tossed from the end of a pier into deep water. This dog did not possess a burning desire to retrieve in the first place. Tossing him into the water was a frightening experience and from this he decided that retrieving in water wasn't all that much fun.

Gus was another client dog that caused me many sleepless nights in an effort to find a way for him to be happy while retrieving in water. His breeding was strictly show lines and there was little desire on Gus' part to retrieve anything. I spent a lot of afternoons walking this dog on a leash through a pond hoping he would relax and become happy. It did not take me long to make a hard decision about this dog. Calling a client on the telephone and explaining to them that their dog will not become a good hunting dog is the hardest thing a trainer does. Gus was an example of a dog with poor breeding as a retriever and he left our kennel for that reason.

Tar was a young enthusiastic retriever when he first came to our kennel. He was quite the alpha always attempting to lead me in our daily training. My solution for his misbehavior was pressure, and lots of it. During his water handling drills, he was especially challenging and constantly questioning my authority. I poured the electric pressure to him and he became compliant. He also learned something I had not thought about, that water was painful. I put so much pressure on this dog around the water that this once enthusiastic puppy was now slinking into the water with both head and tail down. Tar went on to earn a Master Hunting Retriever title but no one enjoyed watching him and I was quite embarrassed to have created this situation.

Other than Gus, the above predicaments could have easily been avoided with proper introduction to water at an early age in the pup's life. Bad experiences in and around water caused Champ and Tar to be afraid of water. When their feet were not touching the bottom they became insecure and worried. This is common for all dogs on their initial swim but should be an afterthought if that first experience is pleasurable.

Before you put any dog in the water, check the temperature and make sure it is not too cold. I cannot tell you what temperature you should look for but anything below 50 degrees is far too cold for a young puppy on his initial swim. How do you get a puppy to go into the water and not be intimidated or worried? You can throw fun bumpers if he is happy about retrieving them or you can walk out into the water yourself and call him to you. I've used both of these successfully many times. However, the most productive way to introduce a young dog to water is with the aid of his mother. All puppies are totally reliant upon their mother for instruction and care. My mother never told me a lie or placed me in a position of jeopardy and for that reason, I trust her completely. So is the case for each puppy and his mother. If there is any way possible, the mother of the litter should introduce the puppies to water by either walking them into shallow water or doing short retrieves in their presence. This works especially well around feeding time when the puppies are hungry. They will follow Mom anywhere in hopes of a meal. Their focus on food will quickly overcome their inhibition to enter water. For this reason, we take all of our litters to a shallow pond and have the mother lead the puppies into the water. We try to do this around age of five weeks and repeat it as often as possible until the puppies go home with their owners.

But what if it is the middle of winter when you get your puppy and the ice will not come off of your ponds until late spring? In this less than ideal situation, you will have to take mom's place by leading pup to water. Hopefully, pup will have formed a strong bond with you and trust you in the same manner he did his mother. Put on your waders and go into the shallow water, calling pup to follow you. If he fails to follow his surrogate mother, coax him by begging and pleading. Take a bumper or bird with you in case you need to entice pup with something other than your companionship. Make it a game by jumping around in excited manner, showing pup how much fun it is to be in the water.

Even with this, some puppies will not get in the water. Is now the time to pick pup up and toss him into the pond? I hope you did not consider this. When all else fails, attach a rope to pup’s collar and lead him into the pond. This needs to be done carefully. Dragging a puppy into the water is not our intention and should be avoided at all cost. Gently pulling a puppy into the water may be necessary and is something I have done many times since ruining Tar years ago. After pup's initial entry, daily repetition of water socialization and water retrieving must be done.

If pup has a strong desire when retrieving fun bumpers, use this motivation as a way to overcome the barrier at the water's edge. Start by tossing a few fun bumpers into shallow wading water. Extend the distance of your throws as pup’s confidence grows until he is swimming with confidence. Move on to deeper water and long throws only after pup has shown that he is comfortable when swimming for bumpers and focused on retrieving. When you have all this in place, the battle is over and it's time to repeat this process on other bodies of water. Be careful when choosing different water in which to work your dog.

Ideal ponds have gradual sloping banks that allow easy entry into the water. Steep banks require pup to jump in the water and start swimming immediately. Save these areas for a later time when pup is confident. Toss your bumpers into the water at 90-degree angles from the bank. If you toss the bumpers at shallow angles, you will be encouraging pup to run up and down the bank instead of into the water. Also, it is not a bad idea to meet your dog at the water's edge when receiving the bumper. Quickly toss him another bumper while both of you are standing in the shallow water making sure you keep an upbeat tone in your voice at all times. Finally, the initial ponds you choose need to be free of vegetation and logs. Heavy cover can be very intimidating and undo a great deal of good will that you worked hard to gain. We will come back to those ponds another day and have lots of fun.

FINISHED DOG

CHAPTER TWELVE

How do you make pup comfortable in a boat?

There is a scene that repeats itself every Fall. It involves the opening day of duck hunting season and hunters with their dogs while traveling by boat to the duck blind. The hunting party arrives at the dock with decoys, guns, coffee, and most importantly dogs. All of this gear, as well as the hunters are crammed into a boat during the early morning darkness. Decoys are loaded first followed by the firearms and coffee canisters. Next, anxious hunters find their places in the boat and the begging for unruly dogs to jump in the boat begins. Pup is standing on the dock above the boat looking at all this mess and wondering if he should enter. The boat is rocking with another dog and the hunters are screaming to get pup in the boat so they can make it to the duck blind before the sun comes up. Pup decides that the truck is a lot safer and more stable than a boat full of idiots so he quickly heads for a secure area. In short order, a good day's hunt is ruined because pup had not been properly socialized to a boat.

The routine of socializing a young dog to a boat can begin at any age. It is preferable to have pup comfortable in water and happily retrieving fun bumpers before starting this process. Begin the game by placing a boat or canoe on land. Make sure it is stable for anyone to enter without rocking or moving around. Place the young dog on a leash and lead him to the boat. If you have already conditioned your obedience commands, use the command "Kennel" to get pup in the boat. However, if your pup has not learned any obedience commands at this time, lead him into the boat with leash pressure or simply pick him up and place him in the boat. Then, stroke pup on his shoulder until you see the desired swallow response. Tell him he is a good dog in an upbeat tone of voice until you can see him relax. Follow this routine with entries and exits in a repetitive fashion at different places around the boat. Pup will eventually become comfortable and happy in the boat because you are there and you have communicated your pleasure with his actions by voice and touch.

If your puppy is an enthusiastic retriever of fun bumpers, use the motivation of retrieving a fun bumper as your primary attraction into the boat. Toss a couple of fun bumpers into each area of the boat and repeat this until pup is bouncing in and out of the boat with no inhibition. Follow those fun bumpers with a few more on the far side of the boat, causing pup to jump in and out of the boat on each retrieve.

Pup should be happy to enter the boat by now with the enticement of a fun bumper. From this point on, start throwing the fun bumpers while you and pup are in the boat on the land. Pup is required to leave the boat to the retrieve the bumper and return back into the boat to you before the game can continue. Move around the boat so pup is entering and leaving from many different spots. He may not want to deliver the first few fun bumpers into the boat, so it may be necessary for you to receive those bumpers outside the boat. You can gradually ask him to deliver all bumpers into the boat after he accepts this new situation.

Now it is time to move your boat to the water's edge and repeat the entire process again. As before, make sure the boat is stable so neither you nor pup takes a dive. Initial retrieves should be done on the land side of the boat and later progress to the water. Shoulder strokes and verbal praise will reassure pup and let him know that you are happy with his actions. This drill will progress very quickly and now it's time for pup to join the Navy.

Wade out into the pond pulling the boat behind you with its new crew aboard. Use a touch on the shoulder and happy voice to reassure pup. Move the boat around the pond until pup is comfortable and wagging his tail about this great new adventure. After he relaxes, join him in the boat and paddle off in search of those dreaded duck pirates. A few trips around the pond should find pup comfortable and ready to retrieve some fun bumpers while at sea. Toss a fun bumper from the boat. If he hesitates to go overboard, you may need to help him into the water. Meet pup at the edge of the boat and receive the bumper before hoisting him back into the boat. Once he figures the process out, pup will try to climb into the boat on his own. Place your hand behind his head and allow him to use your hand as a lever while pulling himself into the boat. It will take only a short time until he prefers being in your boat to sleeping on the living room floor.

From this point forward, pup should travel with you anytime you are in a boat. Family outings on the water need to include pup. Fishing trips with your hunting/fishing partners will serve as excellent venues for new boat and people experiences. Make sure you include pup when it is a time to build or brush your duck blind. The boat ride will prevent that opening morning chaos and a few fun bumpers around the blind will give him a favorable first impression of his new office. Think of the possibilities and include pup at every opportunity.

CHAPTER THIRTEEN

Have you ever seen a gun-shy dog?

I have and it is not a pretty sight. Over the years, clients have brought us ten to fifteen dogs that were mightily worried when a gun was in their presence. These dogs would be perfectly comfortable while retrieving bumpers in a happy fashion until a shotgun came out of its case. At this time, their sympathetic nervous system went into overdrive and shelter was sought. The mood quickly changed from carefree to threatening in the mind of these creatures. What would cause such a reaction?

It is common for people to call us and declare that their dog is not gun shy because they took him out and fired a gun over his head with little or no reaction on pup's part. These people should spend a lot of time in Las Vegas because they are very lucky. I have yet to see a gun-shy dog that was born with this affliction. Gun shyness is caused either by bad luck or poor training. When I was a child, we had a Brittany Spaniel that quickly sought cover when loud noises were present. My father investigated this problem and found that this pup's dog kennel had been struck by lightning when he was very young. This is an example of bad luck and I hope you will never fall into a situation such as this. Poor training is the most likely creator of a nervous dog in the presence of gunfire and, it is always preventable if you know what you're doing. Avoid the " Let me see if I purchased a gun shy dog" mentality by shooting over the dog before he is properly conditioned to handle the "Big Bang".

Proper socialization to gunfire should be handled in the same fashion that we have used and will use in all of our training. Start slow, and proceed at a pace that is comfortable for your dog. You could have the most outstanding retriever on the planet and he would be totally useless if you botch this training routine. Pup must be allowed to accept loud noises on his own terms, so don't be in a hurry.

We have spoken of motivation in previous chapters and now it is time to put that motivation to good use. If we have done our job in conditioning fun bumpers, they should be highly motivating. Feeding time will be a close second on the totem pole of interest to a young dog. When pup is motivated by and focused on another object, it is time to introduce gunfire.

FINISHED DOG

Few things in a seven-week-old puppy's life capture his attention more than the food bowl. So, while his head is in that food bowl, make some loud noises. Banging a few pots or pans, clapping your hands loudly, or slamming a door will create the desired effect. It is imperative that you pay close attention to pup's attitude while any of these situations are occurring. Back away and slow down the process if any nervous responses occur. Creating distance between pup and the loud noise will normally over come his inhibitions. When you find pup's comfort zone, spend a few days at that distance before slowly moving closer. I cannot emphasize the word "slowly" too much when we are discussing this topic.

What if you failed to introduce your young dog to gunfire when he was a puppy? You need to be very careful or this baby might be lost with the wash. If your dog has not been properly introduced to loud noises during his first six months of age, it is advisable for you to delay this process until he is head over heels in love with fun bumpers. While he is chasing fun bumpers you can then add some background noise. Noise comes in many varieties. I prefer to start with a cap pistol and move forward to a primer pistol after pup says he is ready. When pup is comfortable with these noises, we can introduce the report of a shotgun as long as pup is focused on retrieving. It is desirable to start with small gauge guns and later progress slowly to a 12 gauge.

In a later chapter we will discuss placing pup on a chain gang. He will watch other dogs work and develop a great deal of enthusiasm for his work from these observations. Firing a gun while pup is on the chain gang and interested in another dog's actions can serve as a very nice introduction to gunfire. I have done this many times and always been pleased with the end product.

After your dog is comfortable around loud noises, it is time for the two of you to visit a local sporting clays range. You probably need to practice shooting and pup could certainly use the trip to his advantage. This will be another one of his great adventures with you, traveling in a vehicle and hearing loud noises from guns. Start pup some distance from the shooting line and move closer as his attitude allows. In short order, the clays targets will likely gather his attention and any inhibitions about all that gunfire will be an afterthought. Pay very close attention to pup's ears and tail. Move away from the firing line if you see any worry on pup.

This " Big Bang" theory should not be mastered in one day. I have seen many bold dogs that never flinched around close gunfire. But, why gamble? One mistake can lead to twelve years of worry in a dog's life and I don't think you want to take that chance. Your dog will become excited and enthusiastic in the presence of a gun if you take your time and do this properly. Hank was one of my early dogs and he would spin wildly when I appeared with a gun because he thought we were going hunting. To him, that was always fun. I hope your dog thinks like Hank.

CHAPTER FOURTEEN

Have you ever seen a dog give someone the bird?

Oh boy, this conjures up a lot of images in my brain. The bird I'm referring to is a creature with feathers and not a digit on pup's paw. We will deal with the latter part of that sentence in another chapter but, for now, let's discuss introducing birds to our dog in an orderly fashion. Gunfire, water and birds can become objects of great fear to a dog and must be properly introduced at a young age if you desire a finished dog. We have previously discussed gunfire and water, so how do we get a young dog to like birds?

Before we begin discussing the training routine, let's think of reasons why a dog would not like to retrieve birds. My experience with bird shy dogs revolves around two scenarios. First and worst, the puppy has poor natural instincts to chase and retrieve anything. To this dog, birds or anything else are neither interesting nor fun. This guy has little or no chance of becoming a finished dog. The only other reason for a dog to dislike birds comes from a previous bad experience. One of the main causes of a bad experience is too much pressure from the trainer when introducing birds. I have seen this occur when too much mental or physical duress was applied during the force fetch process. Please don't make this mistake. Allow pup to become comfortable with his birds at a pace both of you can accept.

Another example of a bad experience between dog and bird comes as a result of poor shooting. I took my dog, Hank, on his first hunting trip to the eastern shore of Maryland in pursuit of Canada geese. We knocked two birds out of the first flock and I quickly sent Hank to retrieve them. As Hank approached the first goose, it stood up and raised its head in preparation for a conflict with this big yellow dog. My heart sunk when I saw this happen. Hank was a better dog than I had expected and he quickly dispatched the angry bird. I learned a very valuable lesson that day and was quite lucky that my nine-month old puppy was not injured. Had that Canada goose struck Hank in the face with his beak, I likely could have been the owner of a bird shy dog.

All dogs possess a natural instinct to chase and retrieve game. To me, feathered game appears to have a much stronger impact on pup's natural instincts than the furry variety. How do we get our young dog to happily chase and retrieve feathers? From the first day that we have our puppy at home, it is extremely important for us to toss objects for pup to chase and retrieve. One of these objects should be a duck or goose wing. Pup should become very excited and enthusiastic after a few tosses of the wing. Keep a close eye on how pup handles this wing and do not allow him to chew on it. If this occurs, come back to birds and feathers at a later date when you have a little more control over pup's actions through obedience and force fetch training.

In most cases, all goes well when young dogs are asked to retrieve wings. From these wings we will progress to quail and gradually move on to larger birds. All of these early retrieves should be done in the same manner in which we throw fun bumpers. That is, tease pup with these birds and toss them ahead of him enthusiastically. Quail, pigeons, ducks (of all species), pheasants and geese should be introduced in fun manner to your dog when he is physically able to retrieve them. If pup shows any signs of hesitation to chase or retrieve these birds, hustle out there with him and start the teasing process until his interest is high. So what if he doesn’t retrieve them on the first day. Who is in a hurry? Delmar Smith told me many years ago that you cannot train a dog too slowly. When it comes to introducing birds, gunfire and water to your pup, I could not agree more.

Fun birds are now taking the place of fun bumpers on those training days when you use birds. Initially, toss these birds on land so you can help pup with his attitude if his attention should wander. Later, after pup is comfortable retrieving in water, we will toss these fun birds into and across the ponds. Excuse the pun, but now we're killing two birds with one stone, water and bird introduction at the same time.

I have always preferred starting a young dog off with dead birds unless the dog is showing poor interest. When this occurs, it is time to shackle a pigeon or duck and let nature take over. If your dog shows little or no interest in a shackled bird, start looking for another animal in which to pour your emotions and training. Later, shackled birds need to be incorporated into your training program to insure that your dog will pick up and retrieve a crippled bird. This will be necessary for a good hunting dog and mandatory for a finished hunt test or field trial dog. Please be discreet when training your dog with shackled birds, as this can place you in a compromised situation with her neighbors. When you finish this process, pup should be giving you a bird that you enjoy receiving.

CHAPTER FIFTEEN

Why does your pup need to work on a chain gang?

If you should ever find yourself in the vicinity of Terrell, North Carolina, stop by Beaverdam Kennels and visit us. When you pull into the parking lot, look to the left side of the kennel building and there will be ten or twelve dogs attached to a long chain by a series of twelve-inch chains. Some of these chain gang nimrods will be barking and jumping against the restraint with all their might while others will be sitting quietly, seemingly irritated by their noisy neighbors. Many of our new clients see this group of unruly misfits and beg for their dog not to be placed on the chain gang. However, when your dog comes to us that is where his training begins. The most stubborn idiots and the nicest sweethearts all do a little time working on the chain gang. What is the purpose and how can a dog learn anything while stuck on a short piece of chain for a large portion of a day?

Before any on leash obedience work can be done, pup must understand that the leash will control and lead him. This is a hard lesson for some dogs and they will continually pull against a choke chain or pinch collar. If a trainer gives even slightly to this pressure, pup has won a small battle and the alpha position is still open for debate. The chain never gives and most dogs quickly learn that barking and jumping gets them only one thing, very tired. When a pup figures this concept out at his own speed, the on-leash obedience program moves much quicker. Pup has sensitized his neck to leash pressure all by himself. Another prosperous result of the chain gang is that we are not associated with it because all of the action occurs while we are working with other dogs.

A dog will usually remember the last thing that occurred in a certain area and take a guess what that is around the chain gang? Pup's recollection of this "terrible" situation will be of you taking him off the chain and spending some time together. You quickly go from bad guy to hero and this elevated position will gain you great adoration in pup's eyes. It appears that absence does indeed make the heart grow fonder.

The end of the anchor chain broke one day when we were training and I went over to correct the problem.

The free end of the chain gang was moving around when I grabbed the chain and boy, did I get a surprise. The force of ten dogs moving in the same direction at the same time is awesome. I was snatched around by the group and gained a great deal more respect for the power of the chain that morning. The man that introduced me to chain ganging dogs called this theory: power steering. After that morning, I understood why. Three or four dogs moving in one direction will pull the next dog down the line with ease and the concept of following leash pressure instead of fighting it is rapidly accepted. Pup is left to accept this situation at his own pace and you are not the topic of pup's negative thoughts.

One of the convenient things about the chain gang is its ability to be moved and the transferring of the lessons learned also become portable. We chain gang young dogs in the field while running marks and blinds with our older dogs. In this routine, we are given the opportunity to work on several things. An unenthusiastic pup will be motivated while watching kennel mates retrieve in an enjoyable fashion. The excited energy of a motivated dog is contagious and quickly spreads down the chain gang. With this energy comes a lot of noise from the vocal dogs. We call this noisy mass the Beaverdam Choral Group. Fortunately, they never make it on tour as a singing chorus because they soon learn the meaning of the command "Quiet". This set up gives us another opportunity to place pup in a learning situation.

We will discuss drills to gain pup's steadiness later, but the chain gang initiates the young dogs into the routine with no resentment towards you. Pup's first day on the chain is filled with a lot of activity. He will jump and bark excitedly as the duck calls sound, guns fire and marked retrieves hit the ground. After a number of dogs are run, pup will learn that all the birds are not his for the taking and he can only retrieve when you allow him to do so. While this does not complete the steadying process, it sets a nice precedence that pup accepts by his own accord at his own pace. The formal steady program is made much easier by this early chain gang work.

Our discussion thus far has focused on why we use the chain. Now it is time to describe the set up. For the single dog owner, a stake should be secured into the ground deep enough to prevent pup from digging it out. Attach the stake to one end of a twelve-inch long piece of dog chain. The other end of the chain should have a snap swivel that will prevent the chain from becoming twisted as pup moves around. Attach the snap to pup's collar making sure his collar is properly fastened around his neck. We described the correct tightness in one of our previous chapters. If you have more than one dog, the set up is a little more complex. Two anchor points will be necessary and a length of chain needs to be stretched between these points. Attach one piece of twelve-inch long chain (containing a snap swivel) to the anchor chain for each dog that is to be trained. Separate the short chains by enough distance to insure that the dogs attached to these chains cannot come in contact with one another. This is probably the most cost-effective training equipment you will ever possess. It is extremely efficient while being inexpensive to purchase.

FINISHED DOG

The next time you see a group of inmates working along a roadside, I am sure your thoughts will turn to chain gang process I have described. People on chain gangs as well as dogs learn the very valuable lesson of following someone else's lead without challenging the alpha position. It is a wonderful training tool for dogs when used properly. Don't put a striped suit on pup or your neighbors may have *you* arrested.

FINISHED DOG

CHAPTER SIXTEEN

What is an EZ lead and why is it used on dogs?

Every person that professes to be a dog trainer (professional and amateur) looks for an easy way or gimmick when it comes to training equipment. We are such easy targets for marketing departments of companies that carry dog paraphernalia. Each catalogue that arrives at our home is filled with magical quick fix gadgets. For this reason, I have become quite cynical about any product I see advertised or promoted by so-called experts.

I met Delmar Smith in Anoka, Minnesota years ago and it was quite an honor. He had been a guru to me for a long time and shaking his hand was like meeting royalty. At this event, I was hawking videos and Delmar was working the show for several angles. He stopped by my booth and asked me to attend one of his demonstrations. From that day forward, I never saw dogs in the same light.

Delmar was working with pointing breeds and a crowd of around three hundred people was gathered. Attendees of this show are welcome to bring their dogs and there were two German Short Hair Pointers at Delmar's demonstration that had no respect for anyone or anything. He asked the owners if he could use these dogs in his demonstration and they agreed. Delmar slid a piece of rope on the first dog and began walking him around in front the gallery. In a few minutes, the knot head I had been standing beside in the crowd was walking comfortably on lead and standing perfectly still beside the old man without any challenges. Everyone was amazed and he quickly sold every one of the ropes he had brought with him to the show.

When I asked Delmar what was the trick to his performance, he replied in his classic Oklahoma accent, “Piggin’ string”. I had no idea what a piggin’ string was but I knew I needed one. He took one out his pants pocket and showed me how it worked. Delmar had dealt with rodeo stock and horses for a long time so he was quite familiar with this short piece of rope that resembles a choker. I told him I did not care what the cost but I had to have one right now. A twenty-dollar bill later, I was again a kid on Christmas morning with my new toy. There is no doubt in my mind that I have never spent a more productive $20.00 in my life.

Until that day, I had used pinch, choke, nylon and leather collars to control a dog’s actions. All of these had been successful but I was the one having to do all the work by pulling on the leash attached to those collars. There was a jerk on each end of the leash and during our obedience program, we resolved who won the title for being the biggest jerk. After working with a large number of dogs each day, my wrists would become very sore. I was struggling to avoid giving when the pups would pull against me. Mr. Smith and his “Wonder Rope” took all of my discomfort away and made the job of obedience training quite simple.

The key to using an EZ lead is its placement on pup's neck. With pup facing you, form a "P" in your view and a "9" in pup's eyes while sliding the lead over his head. It must remain directly behind pup's ears to function properly. By keeping it in this position, the lead will apply pressure on two bony areas behind the ears. These points of pressure will allow you the ability to totally, and I mean ***totally***, control any dog. It does not matter how big the critter is, he will give to an EZ lead when pressure is applied to the proper areas.

The beauty of the EZ lead is that you do not have to work because pup exerts all the effort. It is as foolproof as anything I have operated in my life and we routinely have small children control large dogs on these leads. Pup must learn to follow your lead before any obedience drills can begin and you can quickly establish the leadership role by simply walking him on the EZ lead. If his chain gang experience when well, then pup should be less likely to fight the leash and obedience will be simple.

When everything is in proper position, pup will be correcting himself instead of you being a jerk on the other end of his leash. After the leash is applied to pup's neck, gather the remaining leash in your left-hand so that you allow a small amount of slack in the leash. When your dog pulls away in an effort to beat the leash, the EZ lead will tighten around his neck and quickly apply pressure to those sensitive areas behind his ears. When he corrects himself and assumes the proper position, all of the pressure goes away. I have yet to work with a dog that did not figure this concept out in one session. Once again, pup will be correcting himself when trying to assume a leadership role with you. By simply holding the leash and maintaining your position, you will develop an alpha role in pup's eyes.

I'm sure you have seen a type of harness that is sold for canine use. It looks to be humane and comfortable for the dog. I feel like it is a little too comfortable and serves little purpose in controlling a dog's actions. All dogs have a sledding mentality and can pull against tremendous restraint with their chests. For this reason, you must make sure the EZ lead never slips down on pup's neck. We have pressure points on our hands that also come in contact with the EZ lead. When pup has the lead low on his neck, the pressure he exerts on our hand will be far greater than the pressure exerted on his neck. In this position, pup becomes the alpha and will lead us where he desires. So, keep the EZ lead in the correct position, behind pup's ears.

When working with an EZ lead, pup learns that following your lead will keep him in a comfortable position. Each time he challenges your lead, the leash will quickly attack his pressure points. It will not take pup long to realize that you did not move when this pressure was applied. His actions alone were the cause of his discomfort. This is a self -limiting process and through consistent work, pup will learn to be responsible for his own actions. Wouldn’t society be better if we could use EZ leads on people?

FINISHED DOG

CHAPTER SEVENTEEN

Who was Ivan Petrovich Pavlov and what does he have to do with a dog learning to be obedient?

For those of you who do remember Mr. Pavlov, please indulge me for a moment. Ivan Pavlov was a scientist who won the 1904 Nobel Prize in physiology for his work with canines and responses that he conditioned into those animals. He would ring a bell prior to feeding the dogs. Later he found that simply ringing the bell would produce the same salivation that occurred when feeding. This salivation response was conditioned into his dogs through repetitive bell ringing and feeding. The term " conditioned response" came from Mr. Pavlov and everyone that trains a dog is forever indebted to him for his work. Conditioned responses to commands are what we strive to attain in all of our training programs and Ivan Pavlov paved the way for us.

So far in our training program, we have a dog that does not fight collar pressure because he spent some time working on the chain gang. He has also learned that an EZ lead will comfortably control his actions as long as he doesn't try to be the leader. If he should fight the EZ lead, he will cause himself discomfort. It is now time to use these skills and help pup learn how to be a good citizen by following a regimented obedience program.

At what age should you start this process? Richard Wolters proved to us that pups are capable of learning their manners as early as the age of eight weeks. His theory was that when a pup recognized their name, it was time to begin some formal training and I agree with this. I have seen many twelve-week-old puppies that listened to their owners very well and were happy to accept the commands of their surrogate moms. Obedience training can begin at any age in life providing the dog is willing to accept the pressure of a leash. My experiences have ranged from six-week-old puppies to five-year-old adult dogs and the results have been pretty much the same.

Dogs see the world in black and white. I am not talking about how they view flowers and the sky but rather, how canines evaluate relationships. To a dog, either you are in control or they are. There is no middle ground. We have emphasized the alpha role in earlier chapters and today is the day you will assume that position. From this point forward, pup will always be beta to you. If you follow our plan, he will accept this role and be comfortable in this relationship.

It is mandatory that you control pup's actions during every training session. Controlling pup during obedience training sessions is accomplished in two ways, the EZ lead and the tone of your voice. While on the EZ lead, pup does not have an opportunity to escape through the mechanisms we described in Chapter One. Bolting, biting and quitting are no longer options to our young student. Our tone of voice will later take the lead's place and we will be able to put the EZ lead away until we train our next dog.

How can we give pup a dose of bitter obedience and make him think that it tastes like sugar? What does pup gain out of doing obedience that would encourage his acceptance of the commands? The answer to both of these questions is a positive reward. This reward should ***never*** be food. A dog that works for food treats is working for himself and that mentality encourages him to challenge the alpha position. Pup should always work for us because we are the most important relationship in his life and pleasing us should be at the top of his priority list. The positive reward a dog appreciates most from a trainer is a thank you in the form of a loving shoulder stroke, affectionate eye contact and a sincere “good dog”. If your dog does not light up on any of those three, you need to reevaluate your relationship. Each command should be followed with a positive reward of some fashion when pup follows our lead.

The first command every dog learns is “No”. Usually a dog will understand this command by the end of his first day with you. It is heard each time pup is doing something wrong and he comprehends this by the way you say “No”. Pup may have been running around the house with your wife’s pantyhose in his mouth or chewing on your prized decoy when he hears that dreadful word. Intonation expresses your feelings to a dog in a language that is universal. The tone of your voice tells pup that he is in trouble and through repetitive use, the word “No” comes to mean the same thing. Voila, our first conditioned response, thank you Mr. Pavlov.

The command "No" means: stop what you are doing immediately. Put yourself in pup's place when he hears this command and understands it. He is thinking that he must quickly stop what he is doing. He would gladly obey you, if he only knew what it was that you desired. For this reason, when pup does stop doing whatever it was that bothered us, we must give him another command expressing what pup can do to please us. ***"No" is always followed with something that will make us happy***. When we are happy, pup will see it through our eyes, feel it by our touch and hear it in our tone. And, that is pup's positive reward. Even when he makes a mistake and is corrected by the word "No", he receives a reward by following our next command. This is a simple method for pup and foolproof for us.

"Here" is the most important command a dog ever learns. It will get him out of almost any trouble that he finds. "Here" tells a dog to come to you immediately and without deviation. This command is very easy for a dog to learn if you will speak his language, Canuus. I have seen a lot of dogs in my life and they all will make a beeline to any person who kneels down and opens up their arms. In this position, we are using postural language to welcome the dog into our presence. While you are kneeling and pup is running to you, add the verbal command “Here.” Cover pup with positive rewards after he comes to you by stroking his shoulder and telling him what a wonderful dog he is.

Let's take a second and discuss how much positive reward to give pup when he follows your commands. Do you remember how a dog communicates to you that he understands and accepts your actions? When a dog swallows, he says, “ I understand.” So, back off the positive rewards when pup says he understands and accepts your thank you by swallowing. Continually stroking pup's shoulder and praising him will eventually lessen the sincerity of your reward and that could be a fatal mistake.

Training pups to come to you with the “Here” command is done with the postural position of kneeling and opening up your arms. After pup has learned this command, add the whistle command of "Tweet-tweet" each time you call him. We start pups on the whistle recall as soon as they are weaned from their mothers. Each time the food bowl goes down, we "Tweet-tweet" on the whistle until the entire litter is feeding. Within a few days, the whistle will quickly gather the litter into a tight group.

This was dramatically demonstrated to us by a pup that had been whelped at our kennel. Shadow went home for a few months but dropped by with her owner one day for a visit. We were in the middle of rebirding the bird throwers when Shadow came running over to me. She wanted to play with the birds and followed the bird boy out to his station. I gave a "Tweet-tweet" on my whistle when she was about one hundred yards away. It was an educational experience for the entire group when Shadow spun around and ran to me as quickly as possible. This puppy had not heard a whistle in two months but the action of returning to my side when she heard "Tweet-tweet" remained as a conditioned response. I use Shadow as an example but we have seen many dogs perform this exact response hundreds of times. Early conditioned responses, good or bad, will remain with the dog for life.

The EZ lead should be used in training pup on the command "Here" as soon as he is comfortable with the lead. Tell pup the verbal command " Here" and apply a slight tug on the EZ lead. Be sure to release the pressure of the lead at the instant he starts coming toward you. Many people will try to maintain leash pressure until pup is at their side. While this works, I feel like it is too much pressure. If pup should hesitate or fail to come directly to you, give another tug with the lead and repeat the command “Here”. When pup arrives at your side, stroke his shoulder until he gives you a swallow response. Pup has learned what we want and now it is time to condition the response with repetition.

“Heel” is a positional command that instructs pup to assume a position beside our leg whether we are walking, standing, running or riding a horse. I receive more telephone calls from people looking for help in teaching their dog to heel properly than any other request. These folks always explain that their puppy is a great dog but he will not walk on his leash. To me, this means that pup feels like he is alpha and should lead his owner where he pleases. I have yet to see a dog that did not learn proper heel position in his first day of training within EZ lead. Place the lead in its proper position behind pup’s ears and began walking forward. If pup should attempt to lead you by moving ahead, simply change direction. The EZ lead will tighten around his neck and he will follow your new direction. It is imperative that no leash pressure be present when pup's head is beside your knee. He will learn this position is safe and causes him no discomfort through repetition. Add the verbal command “Heel” after he assumes the correct position and repeat “ Heel” each time pup’s head is beside your knee.

We have discussed how to correct pup in his attempts to lead us, but what should we do if he tries to lag behind or flop around like a fish instead of following our lead? Keep moving forward and allow the EZ lead to do its job. The important point is for you not to stop moving. If you stop walking to check on pup or coax him forward, the EZ lead will relax and its pressure will stop. He must learn that the only way the pressure around his neck will disappear is by him assuming the correct “Heel” position. With repetition, this position will become a comfort zone. Be careful to not allow this position to become too comfortable for pup. I have seen a few dogs learn that this comfort zone was safer than retrieving.

There has been a recent trend in retriever training for the dogs to become ambidextrous. Some trainers want their dogs to heel on both sides. There are some benefits in this skill but I would caution you to master one side first. Adding the other side at a later time will not be difficult for you and will be much less confusing for your dog.

Our next obedience command will be “Sit”. This command tells pup to sit and remain seated until he receives another command from us. There will be no “Stay” command in this program. “Stay”

is redundant because it means continue sitting and therefore will be deleted from our program. Our EZ lead will apply pressure to the underside of pup's neck when training him to sit. We are now working on a different pressure point. Pull straight up on the lead with your right hand and push down on his butt with your left hand until his bottom hits the ground. Add the verbal command "Sit" and release the pressure on the EZ lead. Pressure from the EZ lead can be omitted when pup is consistently sitting on verbal commands. Later in this chapter, we will get into corrections and the steps you should follow to make things clear for pup. Repeat the "Sit" drill until pup is happily driving nails with his butt.

Most dogs learn how to sit on verbal command in just a few days. As your pup becomes consistent in responding to "Sit", it is time to add a whistle command for sit. It is easy to transfer the conditioned response from verbal to whistle with repetition and patience. Command pup to "Sit" and blow a single blast ("Tweet") on your whistle as he sits. From this point on, you need to mix your verbal and whistle commands so that pup will become reliable with both forms of communication. As before, repetition is the key.

Have you ever seen a dog sit sideways? He flops down and comes to rest on one hip. This is a common occurrence for lazy dogs and needs to be corrected each time one of these sloppy performances occurs. Pull up on the EZ lead until pup sits in a proper fashion. It may become necessary to step forward if your dog will not align himself properly at first. Fight for the proper sit position now and you won't have to address this in the future when you are asking pup to sit on a whistle at a great distance while running a blind retrieve.

Now our pup has learned to come to us, walk comfortably beside us and sit on command. He must concentrate and use his brain as he learns these skills. Pay close attention to pup's focus making sure that the training sessions are not too long in duration. Even though pup's brain is a sponge at this point, it can become over saturated and unable to receive any more constructive information.

In pup's daily routine he will be required to enter many different areas and objects. Airline crates, vehicles, buildings, boats, duck blinds and fenced areas are some places pup may need to be. We will use the command "Kennel" to tell pup to enter what is in front of him. Always use the command "Sit" before you ask a dog to enter. If you give pup a chance to sit and look into the area he is being asked to enter, he will be far more likely perform this skill without a fight. By looking into this area, pup can see that the boogieman is not waiting inside for him.

What should you do if your dog decides that he does not want to enter? You know pup will give to the pressure of an EZ lead, so lead him into the proper area and command "Kennel". Once in the correct place, stroke pup on his shoulder until he gives you his acceptance with a swallow response. Repeat this routine until you start to develop a conditioned response to your command. Some dogs fight this entry with a great deal of vigor. If your pup chooses this option, be sure to maintain leash pressure until you get the desired response. Once he understands that there is no danger in these areas, he will be glad to enter upon command.

At our training facility, the command “Kennel” is learned quicker than any other command. We work in a small aisle way during pup's initial obedience routines. This confined space, along with the mental pressure of training, make pup want to find a sanctuary. When the door of his kennel opens, pup will hurry into his kennel in search of mental relief. We simply add the word “Kennel” as he enters. Within a couple of days this command has become very well conditioned. Think about your individual training situation and see if you can duplicate what I have described with your dog. This can be accomplished by having an airline crate with you while doing pup's obedience routine or working in area close to the entrance of your home.

The next command in our obedience program will be “Down”. This tells pup to lie down and remain in this position until he receives another command. I seldom use this command unless we are relaxing around the home. For this reason, I work on “Down” at night while we are watching television. Command pup to “Sit” and stroke him on the shoulder as he obeys.

Grab his front paws and pull them toward you as you are facing pup. When his chest hits the floor, command "Down" and stroke him on the shoulder again. Most dogs will immediately rise up off the floor assuming a sit position. If this occurs, correct pup with "No" and repeat the "Down" process again. In my experience, it generally takes around three evenings before pup will become comfortable with this routine. But, do not be worried if it takes your dog three weeks.

"Quiet" will be our last command and it is necessary to keep the peace with family and neighbors. All dogs will bark with the correct stimulus so, do not lose your patience when your pup starts. On many occasions, a stern "Quiet" from you will convey to pup that you are not happy with his noise. If he should continue, hold his muzzle and repeat the "Quiet" command. Continued barking will result in pressure on pup's muzzle while commanding, "Quiet" in an angry tone. For the pup that fails to yield these tactics, try a water pistol in his face with each bark while repeating "Quiet". When all else fails, buy an electronic bark collar. They work very well and correct pup instantly.

Pup now has quite a vocabulary. We can stop his actions with the command "No". He will quickly come to us with "Here". Taking pup for a walk is simple because he knows "Heel" and he will sit and remain seated when we use "Sit". Entering a kennel, being quiet or lying down are no longer problems either. It is time to combine several of these commands into a drill that will rapidly speed up the conditioning process.

FINISHED DOG

The "Here"-"Heel"-"Sit" drill will condition these commands and communicate to pup that you or anyone else who picks up the EZ lead will be alpha to him. Start the drill by commanding pup to "Sit" and repeat, "Sit" as you walk away from pup. When you reach the end of the lead, call pup to you with "Here". As he nears you, command "Heel" until he assumes the correct position. While pup is heeling properly finish the routine with the command "Sit". This simple drill will set the stage for all of your future training and who is to be the leader of the pack.

Proper handling of the EZ lead is the key to success with this drill. When calling your dog to you with "Here", your left hand will slide down the lead until you are a few inches from the loop. Grasp the lead with a firm grip as pup nears you and pull your left arm behind you in a sweeping motion commanding "Heel". As pup comes into the correct heel position, pull straight up on the lead with "Sit". Be sure to release the lead pressure when pup's butt hits the floor. If your dog heels on the right, use your right arm. This is awkward at first but will become easy with a little practice.

After you command, "Sit" and walk away from pup, you have the option of going forward or backward. Try to keep balance and pup's life by going in both directions with equal numbers. This drill should be performed in every direction until the conditioning process is well established. How do you know when this occurs? I feel like a dog is well conditioned on the "Here"-"Heel"-"Sit" drill when I can command "Here" and pup will "Heel" and "Sit" in the proper position without another command. This is called chaining, where one command leads to another command without any cues. How do we get a dog to perform this chaining sequence?

In all of our training, we are emphasizing conditioned responses that are the result of repetition. I see a lot of people that believe once a dog learned how to perform a skill, it need not be repeated. I am of the opinion that all of our drill work becomes well conditioned only with ***thousands*** of repetitions. When I tell people to repeat a drill at least a thousand times, they envision this requiring years to finish. If you think about how many times you repeat a command during a drill, it is easy to understand that this volume of repetition can be accomplished quickly. But, it cannot be accomplished in a reasonable time without working your dog on a daily basis. After you have done a thousand repetitions, then it is time to do several thousand more. As Mr. Pavlov proved to us, there is no substitution for repetition.

We have spoken very little about correcting pup for making a mistake up until this time. No dog is perfect and many mistakes are going to occur while training. It is important that you have a method of correcting pup that he understands and is able to comfortably accept. There is a correction system that should be used beginning with your first day. The same correction system will be used for the rest of pup's life whether you are using a leash or electronic collar to correct improper responses.

The system goes as follows:

1) Tell pup a command. If pup obeys, use a positive reward. If pup fails to obey, proceed to step 2.

2) Stop pup's incorrect action with the command “No”. Repeat the command after you get pup's incorrect actions stopped. If pup obeys, use a positive reward. If pup fails to obey, proceed to step 3.
3) Stop pup's incorrect action with the command “No” and use the physical pressure of your EZ lead until the correct response occurs. Immediately release the pressure when pup obeys, repeat the command and praise him with a positive reward.

If you will be consistent in this correction process, the verbal correction of “No” will become exponentially more powerful. Pup will learn through daily usage that if he does not follow your lead after the command “No”, there will be some form of physical pressure (EZ lead or electric). Dogs do not like being corrected anymore than we do. Correction will be a part of their lives and they will accept this correction as long as it is given in a comfortable and systematic fashion. This means you must be consistent and you cannot hurt your dog by hitting, kicking, overstimulating, or jerking him when you become frustrated.

Once your dog has learned the “Here”-“Heel”-“Sit” drill and understands the system of correction we described, anyone can pick up your EZ lead and pup will know they are alpha to him. Each person in the household should take a turn doing obedience work with your dog. Not only does that make life comfortable for the entire family, it makes the world clear in pup's eyes. He will assume the beta position with all of your family and not mind it one bit.

FINISHED DOG

In the first chapter we spoke of displacement behavior and the things a dog will do to avoid giving up his alpha position. Yawning, scratching, sniffing, head shaking and licking are all ways in which a dog will attempt to delay performing a command. In my experience with uncountable dogs, I have yet to see one that did not display at least three of these responses while training with us. Be prepared to correct your dog by way of the correction process if he should exhibit any displacement behavior. Avoid losing your temper by staying focused and having a plan when pup tries one of his tricks. He will quickly recognize that you understand what he is saying and that you are prepared to meet his challenges.

Displacement behavior can be very subtle and is often overlooked by trainers. If allowed to continue, displacement behavior will soon lead to defiance and that may not be quite so easy to correct. Bolting, or running away, needs to be addressed quickly. Keep a lead on your dog if he shows any signs of bolting so you can control his actions and prevent the flight mechanism from being rewarded. If your pup develops a bolting mentality, he is feeling far too much pressure and you need to re-evaluate your training program or your dog. I will be extremely surprised if the problem is with your dog. Bolting usually arises from a trainer attempting to go too far, too fast, too soon. Slowdown the training process when a bolt occurs and take a look at what may have caused pup to bolt. If you can identify the cause, eliminate it from your training program.

Biting is the next form of defiance and is the most worrisome to me. While I have seen a few dogs that are truly mean and look to bite people, this is extremely rare. A dog will not bite unless he feels like there's nowhere to turn except by making you go away from him. We will talk more about biting in our last chapter. If your dog tries to bite you, get some help in the form of another opinion about your dog and your training program.

Quitting or lying down is the last out mechanism to discuss. The dog will quit trying to perform in an effort to get out of his job for three reasons. First, he has little drive or desire to please. This is usually the result of poor breeding or an absence of socialization during the first six months of pup's life. A dog may appear to quit in an effort to con you out of performing. He may lie down on his side and throw the rear leg up in the air assuming a submissive posture. If your dog pulls this stunt, pay close attention to his eyes. If he is looking directly at you, pup is playing the role of the con artist. The final reason a dog would quit is due to too much pressure from the trainer. This pup has given up and is saying that he would rather lie down and take a beating than work in an effort to please his trainer. If your dog chooses to lie down during the training process, you need to pay close attention to yourself and how your dog is being trained.

Most people will confine their training to just a few areas. Pup learns a bad concept when this happens. In his mind, he is not required to be obedient unless he is in one of those training areas. For this reason, you should rotate your training areas to anyplace that pup will be allowed to go. The front yard, garage, great room, backyard, kitchen, bedroom, and deck must all be used as training areas around the home. As pup's ability to retrieve grows, you will be taking him to areas away from your home and he must be obedient in those places also.

Training should also occur at random times during the day rather than before you go to work each morning and immediately after supper each evening. If you have the opportunity to be around your dog throughout the day, ***never miss an opportunity to train***. When you decide to go on a daily walk, take pup along on your EZ lead and do some drill work along the way. After the mailman has filled your box with catalogues, have pup walk with you on leash to the mailbox and perform some “Here”-“Heel”-“Sit” skills along the way. At suppertime, see how long pup will sit in another room while you enjoy your meal. Take a few extra minutes on your trip to the grocery store so that you and pup can sit outside while people walk by you. Think of the opportunities you have during your daily routine that could include pup. Use these times to improve pup's obedience and expand his horizons.

In taking pup to these new areas for training, you are presenting him with many new distractions. Distractions or challenges to pup's conditioned responses are the final phase in the training process. We began with a learning process where we demonstrated what actions went along with certain commands. When pup showed us that he had learned these commands we proceeded to a conditioning phase with lots of repetition. Now this time to see how well conditioned our responses truly are. We do this by bringing in any and all distractions that might catch pup's eye. It seems like every dog will have one or two things in their life that they cannot resist. If you can identify these things with your dog, ask him to perform his drills in the presence of these distractions. Some of the things we use at our kennel for distractions include people, other dogs, birds, cats, children, vehicles, newspapers and bicycles. I have even seen a few dogs become distracted because of the clothes their trainers were wearing. Who says you can't see camouflage?

Upon initial introduction these distractions can become overwhelming. How do we communicate to our dogs that they must remain attentive and under control at all times? We condition this into pup by desensitizing him to those things that gather his attention. Find any object which pup is attracted to and walk him near this object on his EZ lead. Command him to "Sit" in front of the object and back away from pup until you reach the end of the leash. If pup attempts to go toward the distraction, tell him "No"-"Here" and use leash pressure when necessary to pull him off the distraction. As he comes toward you finish the drill with "Heel"- "Sit" and a shoulder stroke. Gradually move closer to the distraction and repeat the drill until pup is almost touching the bait. Don't expect pup accept this in one session. Be patient and allow pup to accept this when he is ready. If you have done your homework and prepared him for this with good drill work on conditioned responses, it will not take very long.

The command "No" now takes on far greater power. Pup has learned that when you say, "No" he can no longer pursue an object of his affections. Coming to you will provide him with security and the comfort of a shoulder stroke. This comfort zone that you developed while pup learned "Heel" has now become far more comfortable for him.

We have covered a lot of obedience in this chapter and it must never be forgotten or overlooked. This training will go on for the duration of the dog's life if only in small doses. Our best field test dogs still get a dose of obedience each day at our kennel. If a dog demonstrates that he is becoming loose in his responses to our commands, we do a little extra obedience with him. In short order, we reestablish the alpha role with a method that pup is comfortable accepting.

Obedience can be overdone and we have seen this on a few occasions. These dogs become stale in their performance and have little energy when it comes time to play. They are trying to avoid correction and appear to be walking on eggs. If you see this in your pup, decrease the number and duration of obedience drills while spending extra time playing together. Strict obedience and a good attitude are two things that can be difficult to keep in balance. Too much work leads to a bad attitude while too much playing leads to poor obedience. Juggle your obedience sessions and play times so that you keep pup's life in balance by having a happy and obedient pup.

All of our work to this point has been on an EZ lead. How do we get our dogs to be just as obedient off leash? Off leash obedience cannot begin until pup is 100% in his performance of the drills on leash. When this occurs, drop the leash from your hand and ask him to perform the drills while dragging the leash behind him. Should he falter, you can quickly pick up the lead and reestablish control. This is where many people get in too big of a hurry. They feel like pup knows what to do and therefore he should be reliable whether he is on the leash or not. Pup's view is that the leash means control and without the leash, he is on his own. So, let him drag the leash around for a week or two until he is bulletproof on his drills.

Usually, I will attach a six to eight foot long thin rope to pup's collar when we are not training with the EZ lead. It is nice to have one for indoors and another for going outside. This keeps a clean rope that can be dragged around the home without soiling carpets, floors or furniture. Make sure the end of the rope does not have a knot in it, allowing the rope to easily follow pup wherever he goes without becoming hung on table legs and such. This rope allows you the ability to get your hands on the dog when he chooses to disobey and attempt an instinctive escape. Running under the table, behind a couch or around a tree will not prove successful as you can grab the leash and show pup the error of his ways. With enough correction, he will understand that commands must be followed. As we stated before, it may take two weeks or two months before pup is trustworthy allowing you take the leash completely off. What's the hurry?

Our next step will be to take the leash off pup completely and hold it in our hand. It is no longer in contact with pup's neck, but it is still in his presence. Spend as much time as is necessary in repeating the drills until pup is once again foolproof without his leash attached. Who cares if this takes an extra month of training? Never forget that no one is keeping score and we can only proceed forward when pup is ready.

FINISHED DOG

The final step is to place the EZ lead in your back pocket. Now it is absent from pup's view and he is totally reliant on conditioned responses, verbal correction and positive reward for his instructions. Pup is capable of squarely facing severe distractions in unfamiliar areas while still giving you control of his actions. If he should never retrieve anything in his life, at least he understands how to be a good citizen and is a pleasure to live with. We have come a long way from Ivan Pavlov ringing a bell to cause a conditioned salivation response in his dogs and we still have a long way to go.

CHAPTER EIGHTEEN

How do you get pup to wag his tail during force fetching?

I am sure that you have met someone who owns a dog and is certain it should not be force fetched because pup is a "natural retriever". Why would anyone not want to force fetch a dog? The most common answer to this question is a lack of knowledge about a method that allows pup to enjoy the process. These people feel like force fetching is cruel and they do not want to subject their dog to such brutality. Or, they may be lazy and have low aspirations for their dog.

Why do we force fetch dogs? To me, force fetching is simply a continuation of obedience training. We force dogs to become obedient with a leash and pressure around the dog's neck. During force fetching, we will force pup to *fetch, hold* and *give* on command. ***This process takes retrieving from being a skill that pup performs when he desires, to being a conditioned response that will be performed on command.*** Our obedience dogs respond to pressure points behind their ears. We will now transfer this pressure point to pup's toe. If we did our job during obedience, pup will understand how to respond to pressure whether it is on his neck or toe.

There is a story I like to tell about my old yellow Labrador, Hank. He needed one more completion to attain his Master Hunting Retriever title. We were at an event in South Carolina and Hank was on top of his game. The final series was a water blind of about 100 yards which required the dog to take an angle entry into the water, cross a pond, angle exit through some cattails and push up a hill to the bird. In watching the other dogs run this series, I understood the hazards because the majority of the dogs required eight to ten whistles to get the bird home. Hank took an impressive initial line and required only two whistles before he was standing over the bird. I was quite proud and relaxed until I saw Hank walk away from the bird without picking it up. I stopped Hank again with the whistle and commanded him to, " Fetch it up". He picked the bird up and started back to me. When he exited the cattails, everyone could see why Hank had balked at picking up the bird. This bird had few feathers left and parts of it were torn open. There was quite a bit of grumbling in the gallery about the condition of this bird, but a consensus opinion came from the group. This situation is one of the reasons why we force fetch dogs. Hank loved to retrieve birds and had never previously refused to pick one up. Had he not been properly force fetched, it is doubtful that he would have earned his Master Hunting Retriever title that day by retrieving this dirty bird on command.

Force fetching in today's training program is a good thing, but it has been thought of as torture in the past. If you ask around, I am sure that you can find a story or two that resemble nightmares from both the dog and trainer perspectives. Neither trainer nor dog enjoyed the process because it was an accepted practice to hurt pup. I saw this become a macho thing with many trainers. They wanted to prove their toughness to pup by forcing this process down his throat without any consideration of pup's perception. Many bloody ears were found on these dogs as a result of too much pressure ranging from a thumbnail to a pair of pliers. Thank goodness our dogs do not have to deal with this any longer, and neither do we.

I have successfully force fetched dogs by many different methods but fell into a groove several years ago. While attending an outdoor show in Minnesota, Delmar Smith and I had supper together a few evenings. We would discuss various training techniques and products over our meals. One evening he asked me how I force fetched dogs and I excitedly opened up my program to him. Delmar looked at me and said, "Son, you're doing it all wrong". I was stunned. Here was the guru of force fetching telling me that I had improperly force fetched hundreds of dogs. I debated this topic with him using the finished product of Master Hunters as my primary piece of evidence. The old man explained to me that my product was good but my method could improve. Until that evening, I was in a comfort zone when training and did not feel like I needed to find a better method. Delmar opened up my mind that evening. Now, I am always in search of a method that is easier and more enjoyable for both trainer and dog. It cost me a steak and shrimp meal for the old man that was followed with a glass of buttermilk, but I was proud to pay for my education that evening.

Preparing a dog for the force fetch program is where many trainers miss the boat. Before force fetching can begin, pup must be relatively obedient on lead, comfortable on the chain gang and head over heels in love with fun bumpers. Pup's on leash obedience demonstrates that he is willing to follow our lead. His comfort on the chain gang tells us that he accepts being restrained and will not fight when tethered. The most important of the three prerequisites is his love for fun bumpers. Should pup lose his focus or enthusiasm at any time during the force fetch program, we can quickly revive him with a few fun bumpers.

Just as pup must be prepared before we can begin, we must prepare ourselves as trainers also. Any loss of focus on the trainer's part or lack of emotional control will result in pup having to pay the price. Keeping a relaxed tone of voice and comfortable posture is mandatory. Screaming will only add more pressure to pup. As with all of our training sessions, a realistic goal needs to be established and worked for. When the goal for that day has been met, it is time to stop. Do not fall into the trap of trying to accomplish too many goals in one day when things are going well because this sets you up for failure. It is important that your goals are easily attainable in the time you have allotted while continuing on the proper path towards a finished dog.

Should you force fetch your own dog or should you find a competent professional trainer to complete this program for you? Until a few years ago, I would have recommended most amateur trainers send their dogs to someone that has force fetched many dogs. The experience that goes along with handling a large volume of dogs is immeasurable when it comes to force fetching. Dogs will give you so many subtle reactions that require quick responses from the trainer. However, I feel comfortable with an amateur trainer completing this routine if he will be patient and remain focused. We have done this many times over the last five years with our on line clients and attained very good results. There will be no timetable or cookbooks in his program. Force fetching usually is completed at our kennel in three to four weeks, but please, do not expect your dog to finish the process in a specific number of days. Pup will tell us how quickly we can move forward.

There are multiple methods of force fetching dogs. All of them involve pressure at some point on pup's body. I have seen force fetching completed by using the pressure from a pinch on pup's toe, ear, flank, nose, and lip. Using either an ear pinch or toe pinch has become the most accepted and successful methods in my view. The trend today is to pinch pup's ear with your thumbnail while placing a bumper in his mouth. This is usually done while you are seated on a bucket as pup stands beside you. While highly successful for well-bred field trial dogs, I do not recommend it for the amateur. This method requires a tremendous amount of physical dexterity and the ability to read very subtle reactions from pup. If your dog has an outstanding pedigree, you are very coordinated, and you can speak Canuus fluently, this method is for you. However, if you cannot answer the above questions properly, we need to take a more conservative approach by using a table and toe pinch method.

By using the table and toe pinch force fetch method, you increase your odds of successfully completing the process because it eases the routine for both you and pup. When pup is placed on a table, there will be no strain placed on your back and you will be much more relaxed. This lack of tension and relaxed manner will make you a better trainer. The table also eliminates each of the out mechanisms pup might try in an attempt to escape our control. To me, using a table makes the trainer's job much easier and I am for anything that makes my life and job easier.

The table we use for force fetching resembles a picnic table with a bar parallel to the surface of the table. The height of the bar above the table should be approximately two inches higher than the height of your dog at his shoulders. Some trainers substitute a cable instead of using a bar, but I prefer a bar for its strength and stability. Initially we will attach pup to the bar with one rope through his collar and another around his waist. Later we will give him more latitude by allowing him to move up and down the bar while still attached with snaps or chains.

Pinching a dog's toe instead of his ear has its benefits also. I have seen many dogs that could withstand a staggering amount of pressure on their ear without giving any response to the trainer. Invariably, these trainers added more pressure to the ear with little success. This led to more pressure and loss of focus by both dog and trainer. I have yet to see a dog that would not give to toe pressure on its initial introduction. Think about that, we have force fetched an unbelievable number of dogs at our kennel using this method and not one of them has failed to give when pressure was applied to their toe *on the first day*. This method is safe because pup will always open his mouth before you can cause any harm. Toe pinch also conditions a muscle response in pup to reach towards his front foot and that is the place where he makes all of his retrieves. How can you argue against a method that is safe for dog and trainer, 100% effective, and conditions the proper muscles?

Now that we have decided upon a method, let's start the training process. At the beginning of each session, pup is placed on an EZ lead and he is asked to perform a few minutes of obedience. This places pup in a position of following our lead and will make the rest of the training much easier for him to accept. After the obedience drill, toss a few fun bumpers until pup is happy and enthusiastic about each retrieve. When you are sure pup's attitude has been adjusted to your satisfaction, put him back on the lead and walk him to the table. Command pup to, "Kennel" while helping him onto the table. Once on the table, pup is to be snugly attached to the bar with a rope through his collar. Pup's rear should also be tethered to the bar by using a rope around his waist.

When we first tether pup to the bar, he will likely become confused and agitated. I have seen dogs violently pull at the bar in an attempt to escape. Some dogs understand they cannot escape because of the time they spent on the chain gang and they attempt to dominate the bar instead of trying to escape from it. These dogs flip upside-down and hang from the bar with their legs, much like a monkey hanging from a tree. My first experience with this was unnerving because I was certain the dog would harm himself. Over the years, I learned to leave these dogs alone and allow them to accept this situation on their own terms when they are ready. All monkeys eventually come down from the tree for a drink of water.

Most dogs will simply stand on the table and wag their tails. They have accepted restraint and our ready to move forward. Regardless of the response your dog displays, do not proceed to the next step until pup is comfortably standing on the table without fighting the bar. This may take five minutes or in the case of head-strong dogs, five days. Many times I will place a dog on the table and leave him there while I work with other dogs, talk on the telephone, or visit with a client. Pup will tell us when we can move on with a relaxed attitude and happy tail. Do not overlook the importance of allowing pup to accept this situation. He will tell you that he accepts by swallowing. Hurrying through this without allowing pup to accept will certainly make your job more difficult in later sessions.

Pup now understands that neither the bar nor table will harm him while they control him. Now it is time to show pup that your hands will not harm him either. This is done by softly rubbing pup with your hands over his entire body. Pay close attention to pup's attitude while you are doing this and count how many times he swallows. Pup will continually tell you that he accepts your touch with constant swallowing. Start at pup's head and work your way down his back. Be sure to cover each leg along with pup's chest and stomach area. Repeat this process until pup is totally relaxed and allows you to hold each of his legs off the table without resistance. While rubbing pup, nurture eye contact by softly talking to him saying, “Good dog”. Watch for the swallows and tail wags. When pup will look you in the eye, wag his tail and not resist you picking up his feet, it is time to move on to the next step.

When I first converted over to this system, people asked me how I was going to sell this program to our clients because it would require more time and therefore, more money. I believed that the clients would gladly pay an extra week or two in training fees if their dogs were happy and I produced the proper results. In reality, this program takes no longer because the back side of the routine goes much quicker. Pup is so willing to accept our offerings that he flies through the rest of the program while wagging his tail.

Now it is time to start messing with pup's mouth by asking him to hold different things in his mouth on command. I like to start with my gloved hand. Pup is not likely to bite me if we have proceeded at the proper pace and he is comfortable with my hands. Place your gloved hand in pup's mouth and hold on to his lower jaw. If he attempts to push your hand out with his tongue or move his head around, simply hold on and talk softly to him with, "Good dog". You will probably be able to feel his attempted swallow response with your hand and you know what that means.

After pup will hold your hand in his mouth without resistance, it is time to replace your hand with a dumbbell. We will use dumbbells initially instead of bumpers just to be on the safe side. Some dogs resent the things we place in their mouths. If we start this process by placing a bumper in pup's mouth, he may decide that bumpers are not that much fun and we can lose some of the enthusiasm towards our fun bumpers. That is not acceptable. Later, we will add bumpers and critters to the process.

Pry pup's mouth open with one hand while placing a dumbbell in his mouth with the other hand. Position the dumbbell behind the canine teeth and release it while closing pup's mouth by applying pressure to his lower jaw with your thumb. Check pup's lips to make sure he is not biting down on them. While maintaining pressure under pup's chin command, "Hold" in a soft voice. Stroke him on the shoulder with your off hand while maintaining good eye contact. Repeat this until there is no resistance from pup. Pup will attempt to swallow and accept even with the dumbbell in his mouth, so watch for this response.

In an ideal world, pup holds onto the dumbbell without any resistance, but there are some dogs that choose a different path. It is common for dogs to swing their heads in an attempt to shake the object out of their mouths. Other dogs will throw their heads back in an attempt to duck away from the mental pressure of this situation. Hold on to both of these guys until they relax while commanding, "Hold" and stroking them on the shoulder. Another normal response is for pup to use his tongue or paws in an attempt to push the dumbbell out of his mouth. This situation is more a more aggressive approach by pup because he feels like he controls anything he can put his paws on. Correct this misbehavior with "No"-"Hold" while holding his jaws in place and stroking pup's shoulder. If this continues, you are going too fast and need to back up until pup relaxes. Remember, it is not a natural process for pup to stand and hold an object in his mouth for an indefinite period of time. Be patient and condition this command with lots of repetition.

From day one, each time you take delivery from pup, command, "Give". This will start while he is a little puppy but will be conditioned during force fetching. Push down and roll the dumbbell back in pup's mouth while commanding "Give" each time you take delivery of the dumbbell. This will have the effect of prying pup's mouth open and condition the muscles in his mouth to open on command. You can further condition this response by holding the jaw in the open position for a short time with the dumbbell and repeating "Give" before taking delivery.

There are a couple of problems that arise while conditioning "Give". The first is lockjaw. Pup refuses to give up the dumbbell even with continued downward pressure and commands. This guy is saying that he owns the dumbbell and is not going to give it up without a fight. Continue downward pressure and repeat, "Give" until he finally releases the dumbbell. His jaw cannot hold out forever, so wait him out. Another similar response is for pup to grab at the dumbbell after releasing it. This is a challenge to you over ownership and you need to emphasize right now that these things belong to you, not pup. If he attempts to grab at the dumbbell after delivery, command "No" and let him know with the tone of your voice that you are not happy with his actions.

Follow each successful "Hold"-"Give" repetition with a stroke on the shoulder and "Good dog" until the desired swallow response occurs. In this, pup will quickly understand what makes you happy and you always finish this unnatural process with a positive reward. It is important to transfer this reward system to the table now. In future steps, we will use it extensively.

FINISHED DOG

After pup will hold and give the dumbbell with ease, it is time to add some distractions and see how well conditioned his responses are. Before we add these hazards, pup must be wagging his tail and not fighting the situation of holding or giving up the dumbbell. While pup is holding the dumbbell, I like to rattle the bar over his head, slap the table or toss a bumper beside him. If he should fail by dropping the bumper, correct him with "No" while placing the bumper back in his mouth with a tap under his chin and "Hold". Repeat these distractions until pup starts to avoid them by looking away when they are presented. Use attrition until he accepts each of these presentations and avoid using heavy tones in your voice or physical correction around his mouth. As he becomes proficient, tease pup with a bird while he is holding a bumper. Gradually add time to the duration of his "Hold" and move away from pup as his skills allow. Each failure will be corrected with "No"-"Hold" and a shoulder stroke until pup wags his tail or exhibits a swallow response.

Now it is time for the fun to begin. Physical pressure to force a dog to open his mouth has been the cause of great debate and is the reason why some feel force fetching should not be done. The key to this debate is the volume and intensity of pressure. ***Our rule on physical pressure is: never use more than the minimum amount required to make pup open his mouth***. This same philosophy will be carried on in all of our future training routines, so etch it in your brain now- use the *minimum* amount of pressure necessary.

If your dog is vocalizing or flopping uncontrollably, you are out of bounds and causing problems instead of solutions. Either of these responses should cause you to back up and reevaluate what you are doing and how fast you are proceeding. Set a goal to ***never*** have pup vocalize during this or any training session.

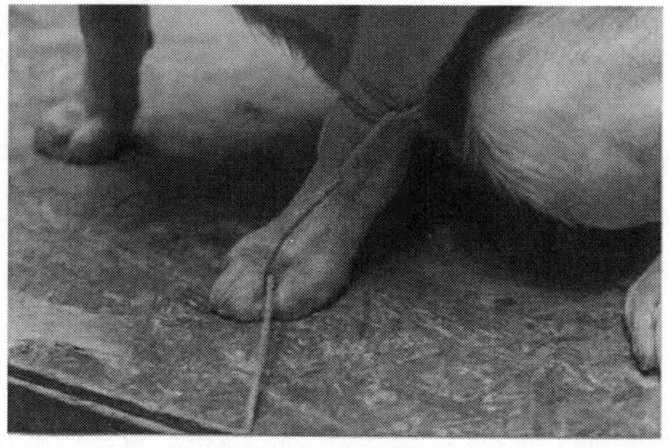

Toe pinch begins with pup tethered to the bar at both ends. Attach a small string (about three feet long) to pup's nearest front leg by using a clove hitch above his wrist. This will serve as an anchor in the beginning and as our only point of contact later. Pull the string down to pup's toes and apply a half hitch around his two middle toes. When you pull on the string, pup's toes should be compressed together. This is similar to placing a pencil between your fingers and squeezing. Before starting the routine, allow pup to accept the string by stroking him until he swallows. He is comfortable with you handling his feet so this should be no problem. Repeat a few "Hold"-"Give" drills if necessary until pup relaxes.

It is time to do the deed, so be resolved to follow this through no matter what response pup displays. Hold a dumbbell in front of pup's mouth with one hand and the string in your other hand. Apply steady pressure to the string until pup opens his mouth. Slide the dumbbell into his mouth and immediately release the string while commanding, "Hold". Put your thumb under pup's chin and stroke him on the shoulder as you softly command, "Hold"-"Good dog"-"Hold". Maintain eye contact so pup can see that you are pleased as well as feel it on his shoulder. On your first day, repeat this three times or until his attitude is positive. I have yet to see a dog that would not open his mouth comfortably and willingly take the dumbbell on the third pull. That is a far cry from what was occurring in this routine just a few years ago. Tortured vocalizations were status quo at many kennels but you should never accept such brutality in your training program. There is no need to hurt your dog in an effort to gain his acceptance of placing an object in his mouth.

What should you do if pup refuses to open his mouth and take the dumbbell? Most people feel like you should add more pressure on the string and increase the discomfort until he complies. Compliance leads to defiance so do not go there. I am of the opinion that we should never add pressure of any type to a dog that is already feeling pressure. Any time pup tells us that a high-pressure front is present, slow down and show him exactly what you want him to do. Therefore, if he should not open his mouth to take the dumbbell on toe pressure, find a helper. Have the helper maintain light toe pressure with the string until you place the dumbbell in pup's mouth with your hands as you did when teaching "Hold". Continue the routine until pup gets the idea and starts to open his mouth.

Pup knows what we want and it is time to repeat the process. Continue until he thinks putting a dumbbell in his mouth is the best thing in the world. Pup will feel this way because of the reward he receives from you after each success. Do not stop until he is wagging his tail enthusiastically while holding the dumbbell. At some point, pup will grab the dumbbell before you can pull on the string. Oh happy day, the most uncomfortable part of our entire training program is now behind us and the rest will be cotton candy, well maybe.

When pup will take the dumbbell in his mouth before we can pull the string, add the command "Fetch" as he takes it. Many people command "Fetch" from the first day when placing an object in pup's mouth or with initial toe/ear pressure. I did this for years and noticed some dogs would flinch on the command "Fetch" because they associated the command with pain or pressure. Adding the verbal command after pup is already performing the skill is passive and allows acceptance of the words instead of fear. Continue commanding "Fetch" while placing the dumbbell in front of pup's mouth until you obtain the desired conditioned response. Each successful "Fetch" will be followed by shoulder strokes, "Hold"-"Good dog"-"Hold" until pup is wagging his tail. Each refusal will be followed with toe pinch and "Fetch" as the dumbbell enters pup's mouth.

Pup is now fetching on command with a happy tail. It is time to remove the rope from his waist and have only his head tethered to the bar. Pup should like this very much and tell you so with a great amount of animation in his body. Up until now, we have held the dumbbell directly in front of pup's mouth and done most of the work for him. From here forward, he must do the work of going to get the dumbbell. Instead of holding it in front of him, hold it a few inches to each side, above his head and below his chin. Pup should now be able to fetch on command around the clock at the distance permitted by the tether. For the rest of pup's life, we will add distance and hazards to this miniature retrieve.

Begin to add some distance by allowing pup to move up and down the bar while keeping his head close to it. I do this with an "O" ring and snap that will travel on the bar with little resistance. Onc end of the snap is attached to the "O" ring and the other to pup's collar. Have pup fetch as before while hooked up to this contraption. Start with a minimum amount of movement by pup and gradually add distance until pup can retrieve from one end of the bar to the other. Hold the dumbbell near the bar while commanding, "Fetch". In short order, pup will be flying up and down the table with the dumbbell in his mouth. If he should falter, use a little toe pressure and adjust the tone of your voice to let pup know you are not happy. Follow all successful retrieves with the proper reward.

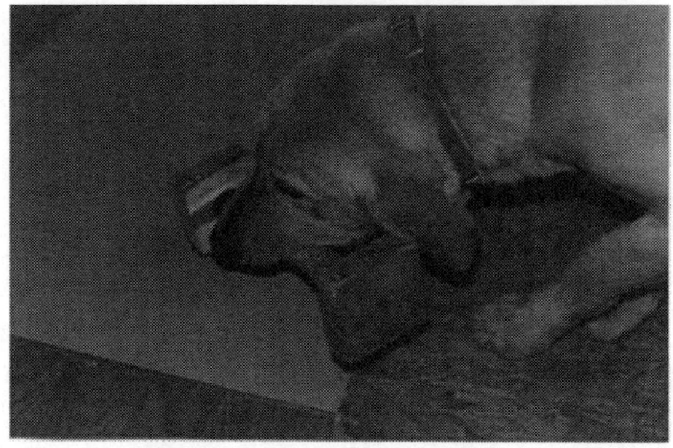

Add more distance to the "O" ring rigging by attaching a chain that will allow pup to reach down to the table's surface. This set up allows pup plenty of latitude and encourages him to move back and forth on the table freely. Gradually move the dumbbell closer to the table as pup's understanding allows. Eventually the dumbbell will reach the table and pup is required to pick it up off the table. Until this point, each of pup's fetches was on an object in our hand. Understand that the first time you remove your hand from the dumbbell pup may balk at his "Fetch" command. This is a new situation to him but will be quickly overcome with repetition and patience. Any refusals to pick up the dumbbell will be followed with a toe pinch and "Fetch". Do not forget the positive rewards.

Decrease the volume of pressure on the string to slight tugs as pup allows. At some point, probably by accident, the string will come off pup's toe and you will get the same conditioned response by pulling on the string attached only to his leg. You may need to go back to pup's toe when pup is feeling bold so, be prepared. When you can place a dumbbell at the end of the table on each side of pup and have him pick each of them up following

"Fetch" with no correction, it is time to put your table away.

Earlier, we discussed what should be done prior to placing pup on the table before each session. That same procedure needs to be repeated after each force fetch session also. As soon as pup leaves the table, toss a few fun bumpers until his attitude is right. Finish the session with some light obedience work before putting pup away.

Following the table work, we transfer our force fetch skills to the ground in a drill termed, walking fetch. Attach pup to an EZ lead and place the string on his leg as before. Several dumbbells should be placed in a triangle about ten yards apart. Heel pup toward each dumbbell, while holding the EZ lead in one hand and, the toe string in the other. Command pup to "Fetch" as you approach each dumbbell and apply some light toe pressure. If our table program went well, pup should pick the dumbbell up off the ground without a problem. Occasionally, a dog will refuse to "Fetch" when he is on the ground. His feet are on the ground and he is feeling somewhat bolder. Use toe pressure and a stern tone of voice to correct refusals. Positive rewards follow successful retrieves.

Move around the triangle until pup is fetching the dumbbells without hesitation. Soon, he will lunge for each dumbbell as you approach it. At this time, you need to substitute bumpers into the triangle in place of the dumbbells. A little toe pressure may be necessary at first, but he will be lunging for them shortly. When pup demonstrates that slight toe pressure by the string will send him lunging for the bumper, try tapping his toe with your foot instead of pulling the string. This will become a useful tool when you take pup to the field and forgot to bring a string along. The status quo method pinches a dog's ear, but we will step on his toe.

After pup has been introduced to birds, they will take the bumper's place. Use each species of fowl that pup might be exposed to in his career. In some cases, a dog will totally refuse the bumpers or birds on the ground. Take these guys back to the table for a day or two and repeat the entire drill with the problem object. This can normally be finished in one session but may need to be repeated for a short time, let pup lead the way. If you are having consistent failures, back up to a point where pup is successful and move forward as pup's confidence grows.

When pup can perform the walking fetch drill consistently, he should be required to hold a bumper in his mouth during all obedience drills. This will condition pup's hold response and reinforce the concept of rapid delivery. It is a good drill to clean up a sloppy mouth where pup continually drops the bumper or shifts it around in his mouth. Use pup's force fetch skills to correct poor performances.

FINISHED DOG

There is one more step left in our force fetch program and many trainers often overlook this important step. Whip fetch is the only time that I condone striking your dog. In this drill, pup will not think you are striking him for punishment but that you are applying pressure to another point on his body in a routine that he already understands. For that reason, you cannot start whip fetch until pup is doing walking fetch without correction.

The set up is identical to walking fetch except you have a short whip in your hand. Walk pup to a bumper and command "Fetch" as he lunges for it. Tap pup lightly on his rear with the whip and immediately repeat "Fetch" again. Some dogs will hesitate or balk if the tap is too heavy so keep it soft. If pup should refuse, go back to your string and apply light toe pressure. Repeat the "Fetch"-tap-"Fetch" sequence about every three to four retrieves. Do not whip fetch on successive retrieves because this is too much pressure and will lead to problems. I also try to avoid tapping on the same bumper twice in the same drill. This can lead to pup developing a hot spot mentality, that is, he thinks the place caused the pressure. Gradually add a little more volume to the tap while being careful of pup's attitude.

Continue this drill until pup is lunging when tapped just as he did early in the walking fetch drill. Any hesitation or looking back at you should be corrected by voice and toe pressure. If this lack of confidence continues, try a few days of walking fetch without any taps and some fun bumpers around the triangle area. Pup's speed to the bumpers will increase as his confidence grows and when he is lunging for the bumper following each tap, it is time to move on.

Before we proceed to our next step, let's take a break and congratulate everyone involved on a job well done. What you and pup have just completed was once thought of as impossible for an amateur trainer. Another myth bites the dust. Spend some time in the field throwing marked retrieves while reinforcing the skills learned during force fetching before starting collar conditioning. Pup needs a break from the mental pressure that accompanies these drills and you need to celebrate what a good trainer you have become.

CHAPTER NINETEEN

Do you want to use an electronic collar while training pup and have him like it?

Using an electronic collar (e-collar) while training a dog has come a great distance from its beginning. My first experience was a nervous and pressure filled time for me more than my dog. I swore that I would never use an e-collar on my dog because it was cruel and unusual punishment. At that time, most people were using e-collars without much regard to how the dog felt. Each time a dog made a mistake, he paid the price. This created a lot of ill will towards e-collars and those people that used them were labeled as tough trainers. I hid my first collar from my wife because I knew she would threaten me with divorce if she thought I was hurting her boy, Hank. It was four months before she found out and I guess I was doing something right because she never noticed any negative change in his attitude.

Many things have changed with e-collar usage since that time from better equipment to simple usage programs. A lot of people still feel like these units should not be used but successful usage depends on the skills of the operator, not the unit. I have never seen a dog that did not accept and happily work while on an EZ lead, but you can also hurt your dog with one if it is used improperly. So is the case with e-collars. You can do an unbelievable amount of damage with an e-collar when you do not know what you are doing or when you fail to control your actions. I can show you how to use an e-collar but I cannot do anything about your emotions. So, before you pull out your charge card and order one of these new quick fix gadgets, make a promise to yourself and to pup that you will always remain focused and in control of your actions when training. If you think an e-collar is not for you, skip to the next chapter where we will show you how to train with or without one from that point forward. However, if you just finished making a promise to your dog, let's talk about the different units that are available before we begin training. In the beginning, e-collars were simple on/off metal boxes that were often unreliable. Today, they are very high tech and several different companies offer excellent models that work at staggering distances over land or in water. I prefer the units that offer variable intensity on the transmitter along with continuous and momentary stimulation choices. You should spend most of your time using momentary stimulation but there may be an occasion where pup is heavily distracted and you need to opt for continuous stimulation, so why not have it available.

Where do we begin with a collar-conditioning program? Pup needs to start wearing an e-collar as soon as he can comfortably support its weight. It is to be worn from that point forward in all of his training sessions. Initially, I like to attach the collar and throw fun bumpers until pup is on the verge of a heart attack. Do this for about a week and pup will think the e-collar means fun bumpers. In my mind, that is a pretty nice first impression. Shortly, pup will be doing airplane spins each time he sees the collar and thinking, "Oh boy, we are getting ready to have some fun". This is an important first step in collar conditioning, pup's acceptance of the e-collar in a fun fashion.

The button pushing process should not begin until pup has completed his force fetch program and is air tight on his obedience drills. We do not want pup guessing what we expect him do when stimulation occurs. He should be performing these skills masterfully in the face of distractions. If we did our homework, pup will have an excellent understanding of what we are asking while being able to process pressure at the same time. Before, pressure was in the form of EZ lead on his neck or pinch on his toe. Now, it will be an electrical nick from the collar. Pup already knows what to do in the face of pressure; we are simply changing the type of pressure. The e-collar will become an infinitely long EZ lead to pup. A nick with the collar will take the place of a tug on the lead. This sounds pretty simple doesn't it?
Keep it that simple and everybody will be happy. In the field, we will only use the collar to correct improper responses that pup has been well conditioned to perform and, it must not be used unless pup has been conditioned to perform that particular skill in the present arena. Do not use the collar to correct responses in an area where pup may have not performed these skills until the training process is finished.

The hardest thing about using an e-collar is finding the proper level of stimulation and sticking with it. Some folks are of the opinion that you should use continuous high-level stimulation until pup complies. There is that word again, compliance. Others think you should use low-level continuous stimulation. I have seen dogs from both programs that look great, but I would not recommend either of these methods to a novice trainer. Likewise, I do not feel like they are easy for the dog to accept. We are not going to teach a dog anything with an e-collar. He will already know what to do; we are going to add electrical pressure to a skill pup can routinely perform.

Our long-term goal with an e-collar is to have pup remain under total control while receiving correction from the collar and understand why the correction occurred. Having pup remain under control is the key phrase in that sentence. A dog that is jumping around or cannot focus on you because he is vocalizing is not under control. If your dog reacts in either of these ways, back off, either you are progressing too fast or your intensity is too high.

I prefer to shop for the correct level of stimulation by starting with the lowest intensity and continue up until I see the acceptance mechanisms appear. This is first introduced during obedience drills. With pup on lead, I call him to me using the lead. After a few successful "Here" routines, apply leash pressure and stimulate at the same time. Look for the swallow response, head drop or neck twitch. Sometimes you can see a change in the breathing pattern. Progress up in intensity until you see pup say, "I accept" with one of these responses. When I see pup drop his head drop or swallow, we are there.

Never take your dog out into the field and stimulate him without first conditioning him to accept and understand the collar. This will take a short period of time but without the conditioning process, pup will be dazed and confused about this discomfort around his neck. I have seen a lot of people strap their new toy on pup and undo a couple of months of good training in just a few minutes by over-stimulating on a correction or correcting when it is not justified. No field corrections should occur until the conditioning process has been successfully completed. The collar conditioning process can be thought of as practice in accepting electrical stimulation. Your football coach didn't send you on the field without practicing the plays and likewise, we do not want to send pup into the field without him understanding how to comfortably accept electrical correction.

Bolting can become a paralyzing side effect of collar conditioning if pup is allowed to move away from your control. Therefore, he must remain on a leash until the conditioning process is finished. Toss a few fun bumpers and have pup perform his obedience drills in the training area while on leash. Make sure pup's attitude is right with a wagging tail. Call him to you with "Here", nick on the correct level watching how pup reacts, and immediately command "Here" again. Reward pup with a stroke on his shoulder and verbal praise. "Here"-nick-"Here" will be repeated three to five times on the first day at various places in the work area while making sure that no two nicks occur at the same spot. Pup will receive at least three nicks but no more than five for the first couple of sessions. If things are going well, go to five. But, if pup is nervous, stop at three. Continue the obedience routine with no stimulation for a little longer. Make sure pup receives his rewards after successful responses. Finish by throwing fun bumpers to each spot where pup received stimulation.

Pay close attention to pup's attitude during this routine. If momentum fades, use fewer nicks and more fun bumpers. Increase the reward by adding a few extra strokes on his shoulder along with a happy voice. Don't be afraid to skip a day if pup shows repeated signs of too much pressure. This is not likely to occur if you are careful, but understand how to overcome it just in case.

As "Here"-nick-"Here" approaches perfection, substitute the whistle for your verbal command. Repeat the same process using only your whistle to call pup. Go forward at a comfortable pace for both you and pup. It is common for amateur trainers to feel more pressure than pup in this early stage so try to relax and make this a game by maintaining an upbeat attitude.

Next, it is time to condition pup to sit and accept a correction while maintaining control in the seated position. The importance of this step cannot be overstated because this method is how we will correct pup for his mistakes in the field. Have pup do a quick obedience drill and command him to "Sit". While he is seated, nick him with the collar and immediately command "Sit" again. If he should move around or get up, replace him in the seated position by using the leash. Reward him on the shoulder and tell pup that he is a good dog. Repeat the "Sit"-nick-"Sit" five to seven times per session. As before, move around so you do not stimulate pup at any spot more than once. Use a positive reward after each successful nick.

Pup should know how to sit on a "Tweet" with the whistle. Now, substitute "Tweet" for "Sit" and repeat the drill. Spend a lot of time conditioning "Tweet"-nick-"Tweet" as you will use this for the rest of pup's life. It is common for us to repeat this routine for several days with a dog, almost to a point of boredom. I want pup to completely understand that remaining seated while being stimulated and following my next command will always gain him a positive reward. I might use a stroke of the shoulder or fun bumper now, but later he will get to pick up a bird when he follows my lead in the field. With time, this bird will become pup's greatest reward in life.

Pup learned to heel beside us early in the program and transferring this command to e-collar correction is simple. Walk pup on leash and change directions. As the leash tightens command, "Heel", nick pup with the collar and command "Heel" again. It is important to apply the nick at the same time that the leash is tight around pup's neck instead of while he is coming to you. Reward pup with verbal praise and a stroke on his shoulder until he says, "Thank you, I understand" with a swallow. Repeat this routine as you walk together or as you face each other. When you face each other, it quickly conditions the flip response everyone likes to see as pup delivers a bird or bumper. As his proficiency grows, ask him to do this while carrying a bumper.

Pup is now conditioned to accept the e-collar while coming, heeling, or sitting with voice or whistle. It is time to mix the commands into a full "Here"-"Heel"-"Sit" drill. Use your nick at varying times as pup allows and as before, avoid successive nicks or multiple nicks in the same area. You can increase the number of nicks as long as you pay close attention to pup's attitude. Toss a few fun bumpers when necessary and pour on the positive rewards as needed. Don't forget to use both voice and whistle commands during the routines.

Following a successful obedience conditioning process, it is time to condition pup to fetch with the e-collar. This drill is commonly called walking electric fetch. We want to take the skills learned during walking fetch/whip fetch and repeat them using the e-collar instead of toe or whip pressure. Pup already knows the routine; all we are doing is substituting the point and type of pressure. Your job as a trainer in this drill is to make sure an acceptable level of stimulation is used and most importantly, pup maintains a good attitude during his work.

Walking electric fetch is always started with a few fun bumpers. This adjusts pup's attitude to a positive level and opens his acceptance channels. Spread several bumpers into a triangle and walk pup on leash around the triangle repeating the walking fetch routine until pup is lunging for each bumper. Then repeat this with a short session of whip fetch. Now we are ready to electrically condition "Fetch" by walking pup to a bumper commanding, "Fetch", applying a nick with the collar, and commanding "Fetch" again. "Fetch"-nick-"Fetch" should be repeated three to four times during this initial session. In the beginning, never nick on the same bumper in a session. Likewise, space your nicks four fetches apart by going completely around the triangle and fetching each bumper before using "Fetch"-nick-"Fetch" again. This should prevent pup from flaring from an area where he is feeling too much pressure and decrease the hot spot/bolting mentality. Any flaring should be met with a multitude of fun bumpers into that area so pup learns that the area did not cause him any problems.

There is no time frame in walking electric fetch. We must proceed at a pace that is comfortable for both student and instructor. With some dogs, I might skip a day or two while others may need to repeat this drill every day. Let pup tell you how often you should repeat walking electric fetch with his attitude and willingness to please you in the drill.

Occasionally, a dog will balk or hesitate when you apply electrical pressure in the fetch drill. Pay close attention if this occurs. Pup may be confused if the other drills did not go well or he may be feeling too much pressure from the e-collar. Some dogs need to go back to the table and repeat those steps using electrical pressure instead of toe pressure. While this is rare, if your walking electric fetch drill is filled with refusals, do not be afraid to put pup back up on the table. He knows the rules on the table and his ability to accept this new pressure will be greatly increased.

When walking electric fetch is going well, you need to condition pup to accept electrical stimulation while he is carrying a bumper in his mouth. Have pup fetch a bumper off the ground and carry it while heeling beside you. Seat him with a "Tweet" from your whistle. As he settles nick him with the e-collar and repeat "Tweet" again with your whistle. Should he spit the bumper out, command him to "Fetch" and repeat the routine until he gets the idea. Do not forget to give him a positive reward when he does this properly. Next, call pup to you with "Tweet, tweet"-nick-"Tweet, tweet" while he is carrying the bumper. If pup drops the bumper, take him back to it and have him fetch it up on command. Now we are mixing our obedience and walking electric fetch lessons in to one drill. These skills will become very important later in a handling drill where pup is asked to accept correction for poor casts while handling on the return in Double-T.

Our next step in collar conditioning is to stimulate pup on his path to retrieve while he is moving some distance away from us. Instead of pup being by our side, he can now be any distance from us. This drill has been termed forcing to the pile because you continually send pup to the same pile of bumpers and add electrical force while he is moving. Pup may have been a picture of perfection by our side but a little distance can create just enough freedom to invite our student to become unreliable.

I like to begin the drill by placing a group of bumpers (10 or more) about 15 to 20 yards away in plain view. A mowed yard works well for this drill. Toss a fun bumper or two to the pile to show pup where you want him to go. When his attitude is right, line him up facing the pile and send him to retrieve a bumper with the command "Fetch". If he hesitates, move closer and repeat, "Fetch" until he goes eagerly to the pile. Continue to send him until his tail is wagging his entire body. Follow each successful retrieve with a positive reward. Now send him with "Fetch" and when he is about half way to the pile, nick him the collar and repeat, "Fetch". If he should stop or hesitate, repeat, "Fetch" until he goes on to the pile. In some cases, you may need to toss a bumper to the pile to get pup moving. If this happens to you, stop what you doing and go back to previous drills because pup is not ready to be forced to a pile. However, if pup accepts the nick without a problem continue the "Fetch"-nick-"Fetch" routine on every fourth or fifth retrieve. Nick pup from one end of the line to the pile to the other. That is, nick him as he leaves you, while he is half way, and just as he is about to pick up the bumper (not on the same retrieve). Cover the entire line to the pile over a period of days so that pup learns to move freely from you all the way to the bumper pile. When pup is eagerly retrieving each bumper from the pile with or without stimulation, our job is done.

We spoke earlier of an out response that dogs use in an effort to escape our control. Bolting from electrical pressure has been a common response from a pup that has not been properly conditioned or when a trainer is using too intense a level of stimulation. In both cases, pup is no longer trying to work with the trainer. His focus is on getting away from the heat instead of on what you want. If this happens, stop what you are doing and evaluate where both you and pup are at in the program. Most bolting dogs will display this tendency early in their training, perhaps when they are small puppies. Being patient and going slowly will greatly decrease the chances of your dog choosing the bolt option.

However, some dogs choose to bolt no matter how well we prepare them and unfortunately, they must be de-bolted. This involves a fair amount of electrical and mental pressure and, demands that a leash be attached to pup so you maintain total control of his actions. A bolting dog will attempt to go to a safe spot or sanctuary. This may be the truck, kennel, woods, pond, or neighbor's house. I have seen dogs try each of these options in the past.

The idea behind de-bolting is for pup to feel more pressure at spot where he wants to go, than where you want him to be. Pup will show you where he wants to hide so let him go there. When he gets comfortable in that spot, attach his leash and call him out of his comfort zone with "Here". A tug on the leash may be necessary if pup decides to fight your control. Stroke him on the shoulder and let him know that coming to you is better than bolting away. Allow pup to go back into his comfort zone and call him out with "Here"-nick-"Here" this time. Repeat this routine a few times until pup is hesitant to go back into his comfort zone. Then command him to "Kennel" back into that area and call him out with "Here"-nick-"Here". Repeat this sequence mixing electrical stimulation one time with no electrical pressure the next until pup is moving freely away from his sanctuary.

Hopefully, you will not have to go through this but one time. After pup learns the process, de-bolting from any area or place should be a little easier. If continued bolting does occur, you have a problem in your training program and this needs to be evaluated by someone with plenty of experience. Whether you seek advice from a well-versed amateur or a professional trainer, do not be afraid to ask for help. It is amazing what another set of eyes will see while our attention is focused elsewhere.

You might find that pup may require more than one level of stimulation in different situations. If the distraction in front of pup is large enough, you will probably need a little more juice. This is very common when you go to the field and start using the e-collar. Pup may have been a textbook case of perfection in the yard drills but acts as if the collar is turned off when you stimulate him in the field. Dogs will adjust their tolerance of the e-collar to the distraction in front of them. If your dog is comfortable on a level #3 in the yard, it would not surprise me if he required a level #4 or #5 to stop him from chasing a fleeing deer. This is why I prefer variable intensity on the transmitter instead of on the collar. Do not let your dog's level of stimulation be etched in stone. Instead, roll with the flow by paying attention to how motivated pup becomes with each distraction and most importantly, to how pup accepts the new level of stimulation.

This chapter has scrambled a lot of people's brains in the past because they went too fast or skipped steps along the way. Nothing we have discussed is difficult for a knowledgeable trainer to understand. Likewise, it is easy for pup to understand and accept as long as you proceed in an orderly and comfortable pace. So, take your time and have a little fun along the way. Keep pup's tail wagging with plenty of fun bumpers. You will find the excitement pup displays when he sees his collar is contagious. If you use your positive rewards when pup does well, then both of you will look forward to training with an electronic collar.

CHAPTER TWENTY

How does pup learn good marking skills and why can't you do this by yourself?

Have you ever been to a field trial or hunt test and watched the dogs at those events? I suggest that you take part of one Saturday and spend some time watching how well trained our dogs can become. It is impressive to see the dogs maintain total control while being handled a great distances on blind retrieves. But, the most mind boggling skill I see displayed every weekend is the precision with which those same dogs mark and remember the fall of several birds. A short distance may be all that separates two marked birds but pup will dig those marks out with little effort when properly trained.

The ability to remember where a bird fell and go directly to that spot is an extremely important skill to the person who wishes to run his dog in retriever events as well as to the average hunter in a dove field or duck marsh. In both cases, the dog is expected to locate the game quickly without disturbing too much surrounding area and return directly to the handler. Such skills will earn a nice score at the event and allow the hunter to continue his pursuit of game with no wasted time or energy. So, how does pup learn to be a precise marker?

Marking skills are dependent on many different complex traits that are genetically passed on to pup by his ancestors. We as trainers can nurture these traits with our training program but we cannot instill them if they are not already there. For that reason, if your pup is struggling with his marks after having been properly brought through a training program, he may not be a good candidate for retriever events that demand precise marking skills. You can compensate for poor marking by developing a dog that handles well in the hunting arena but this will be the kiss of death at field trials. Let's discuss these traits and see how we can wake up those genes in our dog's champion pedigree.

The first thing I look for when working with a pup on his marks is focus. When retrieving, some dogs would rather smell the flowers and look behind each bush than remain focused on where the bird fell. Other dogs rarely see anything but the bird and jumping over a hedgerow or running through heavy cover is no problem. They become so focused on that prize in field that their senses are oblivious to everything else. Motivation to chase game and the ability to focus are tightly intertwined. Focus can be nurtured through simple short retrieves in clean areas that offer little distraction.

Do any of you wear reading glasses? Imagine taking your glasses off and being asked to read a complex legal contract. This is how some dogs feel since we cannot outfit them with corrective lenses. They were born with bad eyesight and, as of this printing little can be done about this problem. Repetitive marking drills will help pup compensate for his anatomic problem, but his vision will never be the same as a dog with excellent visual acuity. You can decrease the odds of not having to deal with this problem by researching your puppy before purchasing. There is no guarantee that your pup will have perfect eyesight but checking the parents and grandparents with the Canine Eye Research Foundation (CERF) will help your chances.

Some dogs, like people, are just smarter than others and they have a heightened ability to remember. It could be which flowerbed they buried a bone in or which bush a bird fell behind 300 yards away. Memory is a skill that relates to pup's IQ but can definitely be improved through repetitive training. I have worked with a few dogs that were able to run triple marked retrieves on their first day. These pups were rocket scientists to me because they possessed the ability to remember exactly where birds fell, what time of day they were fed or which box on the truck they rode in without any help from me. And then there are dogs that are dullards requiring constant repetition to jog their memories. Continual maintenance is required to keep them on the same page as the rest of the class.

Even dogs with excellent memories miss their marks and at that point, perseverance takes over. A dog that stays in an area and hunts for an extended time without returning to the handler is well blessed with perseverance. This dog is not quick to give up his chase because he trusts his eyes and memory. Perseverance is born into most dogs but can be nurtured by making sure pup is successful each time he goes into the field for a retrieve.

Some dogs possess all the skills we have discussed thus far and still struggle to mark well due to a lack of desire. They see the bird fall with no trouble, remember exactly which blade of grass it hit, stay in the area of the fall and remain focused until the retrieve is completed. The problem is that pup walks all the way out to the bird because he lacks a strong desire to retrieve. This is no big deal for short simple retrieves but as the distractions and distances grow, things become a little more complex. Pup's heart is not into his work. We spoke about a lack of desire in earlier chapters, so I will not rehash that topic again. Start looking for another dog.

Mental focus, visual acuity, memory, perseverance, and desire all create a confident personality in pup. And in my experience, a dog's ability to mark is directly related to his confidence in himself. Richard Wolters' last dog was named, Duck, and he spent the better part of three years with me in training. His personality was quite bold and the Duckster was never short on confidence in himself. For this reason, he was an incredible marker. In the years that I handled Duck, I can only remember one incidence where he required help from me to find a marked retrieve. Think about that, one handle in three years of hunt testing and daily training. Duck was so confident in himself that he never questioned the location of a bird; he knew where it was. I will always smile when I think of Duck because it makes me feel good thinking about a dog or person with that much confidence in their work. To this day, RAW's Southland Duck Soup, a.k.a. Duck, is the best physical specimen of a Labrador Retriever that I have seen.

So, we understand what makes pup mark well, how do we work on these traits and bring them to their fullest potential? It all begins when you bring pup home and throw things for him to retrieve. Fun bumpers start the process by building desire and mental focus. They also help pup's eyes start to focus at varying distances. An eight-week-old pup can see clearly only a short distance. With age and practice, canine vision improves to the point where a hunting dog can see birds in flight long before his master in the duck blind knows they are there.

Fun bumpers do little for memory and perseverance so how do we arrange our training program to develop the confidence we require for a dog to mark well? There is one cardinal rule in this marking program; **PUP MUST NEVER RETURN FROM A MARKED RETRIEVE WITHOUT HIS BIRD OR BUMPER!** I do not care what it requires from you or your training buddies, pup must always find his mark and return with it. Put yourself in pup's place. If you were successful at your job each day, how confident would you become in your approach to work? It is well documented that a confident dog marks well and the best way to build confidence is through successful retrieving. If pup fails to find a fun bumper, walk him out to the area and stay there with him until he finds the bumper and picks it up.

Pup will be required to mark a varying distances over his life and we can only throw bumpers a short distance. It is mandatory that pup be able to mark well at whatever distance your individual needs may require. He is capable of marking at whatever distance you train him, so set your training goals accordingly. The average hunting dog should be proficient at approximately 150 yards. A licensed field trail dog needs to stretch that distance out to around 450 yards. On my best days, I can throw a bumper around 60 yards. So, I need help in the form of a thrower that can be located at whatever distance is required.

The thrower can be a launcher that will toss a bumper when you press a button on your transmitter. It also can be a launcher that propels a bumper from a pistol or rifle at your side. You could walk out into the field, throw the bumper, walk back to pup, and send him to retrieve. I know people that use each of these methods for stretching the distance on marked retrieves. There is one major problem with each of these methods; if pup fails to find his mark, we have no way to help him out of his predicament. Sure, we can walk him out to the area of the fall but momentum and confidence will be lost over the long distance.

I have done each of the things mentioned in the previous paragraph with moderate success. However, if I cannot have a person throwing bumpers or birds for marked retrieves, I work on something else until help is available. Having a helper or training partner is beneficial in many ways. First, they give you another view of what is happening during the training session. Often, people are too close to recognize problems that are occurring. We all need a little pat on the back on both good and bad days. Training partners are usually your best cheerleaders because they see how much effort is going into the finished product. They also motivate you to get off the couch and go train. If you do not feel like training today but you know you buddy needs to prepare for an event coming up next week, you will go out and help him. While helping a friend, your pup will also get some work on an otherwise lost day.

The most important function of having a training partner is to help pup if he should fail to find a marked retrieve. The primary focus of a thrower is to keep pup's attention in the area of the fallen bumper or bird until pup finds it on his own. When a pup falters on his mark, the helper should call pup into the area of the mark with "Hup, hup, hup". Pup associates "Hup, hup,hup" with fun bumpers and will likely rush toward the helper. At this point, the helper must keep the bumper or bird between himself and pup so when pup moves to the helper, he will find the bumper. We do not want the helper to stand beside the bumper and have pup find it at our helper's feet. This could encourage pup to go the bird thrower when he loses his mark in the future. So, your helper needs to be able to read when a dog requires help as well as dance around the field while keeping pup in the proper position.

We know how to guarantee success on each retrieve, how do we start the training program while using our helper? The helper should go into the field a short distance and get pup's attention by calling "Hup,hup,hup". As pup focuses on the attention and takes off for his fun retrieve, your helper should throw the bumper or bird into a clean area with little cover or hazards. If you paid attention to what I was saying, you noticed that we let pup break before being released to retrieve. Steadiness will come later. Our goal now is to have pup cover the distance we have set up and be successful by finding and retrieving the bumper.

Some pups may lose their focus when they reach the distance they have been previously conditioned to retrieve during fun bumpers (30-40 yards). For these problem students, the helper may need to "Hup,hup,hup" pup continuously from the time pup leaves the handler until he finds his reward in the field. Start short and keep the retrieves simple until pup shows that he can carry some distance with ease. As his skills grow, add more distance and begin incorporating a few hazards between pup and the bumper. Initially, I place the birds in plain view but later I will conceal them in cover. And in case you do not already know, use white or black bumpers. The contrasting shades are seen well by pup. We will use the orange versions later during our handling routines.

I prefer to start the marking process on land to insure pup's success. It is a whole lot easier for our helper to run out into the field and help pup than swim out into the pond, so let's master the land skills before heading to water. After land is going well, repeat the entire routine on water. Let pup break now so his momentum will stay high. While at water, make sure the entries and exits from the ponds are squared off (90 degrees). Asking a pup to take angles into or out of the water is not easy and could create a bank running problem that might be difficult to correct in the future. We will introduce all the angles when pup proves that he is reliable.

FINISHED DOG

CHAPTER TWENTY-ONE

What is the best way to steady pup without losing any desire?

Each week I receive telephone calls from amateur trainers talking about their 16 week-old puppy that is already steady to wing, shot and fall. This always worries me. How much desire was taken out those youngsters in an attempt to gain too much control too soon in their training careers? Most inexperienced trainers place a tremendous amount of emphasis on a dog being totally steady and this becomes one of their primary training goals. A lot of desire and enthusiasm is lost when this happens.

I am of the opinion that we should not steady dogs until they approach eight to twelve months in age and, then only if they are motivated retrievers. Think about the steadying process from pup's view. He is sitting there ready to run through anything in pursuit of a bird or bumper. But you tell him, "No, don't chase that object, sit beside me without moving". If this scenario is repeated too many times, pup may begin to think that sitting still is more important than chasing and retrieving. That is the last thing I want my pup thinking.

There are training programs out there that will show you how to steady pup in two to three days. For the right dog, these programs work very well but for the other ninety percent, this style of training can be the kiss of death. Why hurry this process and risk damaging one of pup's most important instincts; the desire to retrieve? Be patient and allow pup to accept each of the steps in the program at his own pace. This will prevent any loss of enthusiasm towards retrieving and it will also take the pressure off you to meet a timetable.

Pup should learn how to become steady during marking drills. We run our young dogs on a short (six foot) check cord when they first go to the field. This allows us control over them for those first sessions in case the temptations of open spaces are too great. The rope helps us to gather pup into our side when he returns from a retrieve. He thinks the EZ lead is attached to him and that dictates control. A check cord also gives us control over pup before we send him on his retrieves and that is how we start the steadying process. I can see some of you thinking about running your pup on a check cord and worrying about him being injured if the cord becomes tangled. I have done this for many years and as of today, there has been no harm come to any dog from a rope.

In our last chapter we talked about pup running freely on retrieves out to whatever distance our goals require with the assistance of a bird thrower. The responsibilities of the thrower now grow as pup learns to become steady. It is likely for a young dog to bounce around at the line when being restrained in our initial sessions. If our helper throws his bird while pup is looking back at the handler because of the tension on the check cord, our student may not see the mark and will struggle to make the retrieve. So, the thrower must make sure that pup is looking directly at him before tossing his bird. A bigger responsibility will come after pup does learn to sit still. Should pup break after his bird before being sent to retrieve, it is the thrower's job to hustle over to the bird and pick it up before pup gets to the bird. That will be sufficient punishment to our student in the first few sessions. If pup goes before being released, he does not get his reward of the bird.

With pup on his check cord at your side, command him to "Sit" and signal your helper that you are ready. Your helper should blow a duck call, fire a gun and/or yell toward you to gain pup's attention. Repeat "Sit" as your helper throws the bird and again when the bird hits the ground. Pup will likely be attempting to fight your restraint at this point and you need let him know he is being good. Stroke his shoulder and repeat "Sit" again. Watch for pup to swallow and say, "I accept". Release him to retrieve by saying his name and watch the enthusiasm pup displays. Gradually hold pup longer and longer until the day comes where he does not attempt to pull against the check cord. He understands and will tell you so with a swallow or two, so pay attention.

You are going to tell pup "Sit" four times on these initial retrieves; before you signal your helper, while the bird is in the air, as the bird hits the ground, and after the bird has stopped moving. In this, you are communicating to pup that you would like for him to sit and remain seated after each of these occurances. Your safety net is the check cord. As long as you hold onto it, pup will stay under your control so do not let go until you send him to retrieve. The final safety feature is your helper. He will not allow pup to gain a reward if he should break to retrieve before hearing his name. If pup should escape your control and attempt to retrieve before being sent, call him back to you and repeat the routine until he performs it correctly.

Why do we say pup's name to send him for a retrieve? Imagine you and a buddy out hunting ducks together. Both of your dogs are well-oiled machines sitting perfectly still outside the blind. You shoot a single mallard before your partner can pick up his gun because he was eating a ham biscuit. If both dogs were trained to go retrieve on the universal retrieving command "Fetch", we are likely to have a dog fight and very little bird left for supper when you utter that word. But, if both dogs were conditioned to pick up things they see fall (marked retrieves) when hearing their name, then all is well and you can select which dog you want to retrieve. What are the chances of you and your partner choosing the same names for your dogs? It looks like you might be having roasted mallard after all.

The steadying process normally takes us two to three weeks to complete at our kennel. Do not etch that time in stone for your dog because he may need a few extra days or weeks. Once again, let him settle into this at his own pace. You are going from a wild little puppy that breaks on your helper's first sound to a dog that will sit motionless through a lot of commotion until you send him. There is a lot of acceptance that must be allowed to happen if pup is to keep a strong desire to retrieve. So, watch for the swallows. He will tell you in his language when things are right.

What if you were a little zealous in your training and sped the process up to a point where pup does think sitting still is more important than going to retrieve? These are called "No goes" and I hope they scare the wits out of you. They mean something is wrong with your training program and you need to figure out what is the problem. Pup will no-go for one of two reasons; defiance or lack of confidence.

The defiant dog will lock onto the mark and remain focused on it but not budge when his named is called. He should be corrected by walking him out to the bird and reminding him that you still remember what he learned during force fetching with a tap on his toe or nick with the collar. This will pass as pup accepts your alpha role in the field, so use the tools in your toolbox.

Some pups will look worried during this routine with pinned ears and lowered heads. They might swing their heads side to side after the bird is on the ground. These guys are about to explode under the pressure so relieve that anxiety by going back to fun bumpers. Let pup break again as your helper hup's him out to his marks. Repeat these carefree sessions until pup's attitude is back to an enthusiastic level and revisit the steadying process at a later date.

Once pup learns how to remain steady, his life has changed. From this point forward you will dictate when he can retrieve. "Hup, hup, hup" tells him to chase at his own pace. But, "Sit" places pup in a situation where he must remain motionless unless his named is heard. This sounds great but guess what? Even after this training routine, pup *is* going to break every once in a while. As a matter of fact, I want him to try me. If a dog does not want a bird badly enough to challenge me by breaking for it, then I don't have much respect for him or want him as my hunting dog. This leads us to how we correct pup when he just cannot stand it and takes off after a bird on his own.

For the trainer that is not using an e-collar, stop pup's intent to retrieve with a resounding "NO!" As pup slows or stops his forward progress, call him back to you with

"Here"-"Heel" and a demonstrative "SIT!" Repeat, "Sit" in a firm tone and ask your helper to throw the bird again. Pup will be corrected by the tone of your voice and you not allowing him to pick up his prized bird. This is a self-limiting process because pup will eventually learn that each time he goes before being sent, he gets no positive reward from you or from the bird.

If you are an e-collar user and have finished the conditioning process, use the same procedure as above to stop pup and get him back to you. Instead of saying, "Sit", use "Sit"-nick-"Sit" as he comes to your side. Repeat "Sit"-nick-"Sit" again as you signal your helper to throw his mark again. It is important that you correct pup at the spot where he made his mistake and not out in the field. He will understand and accept the correction a lot quicker if it occurs at the spot from where he broke. Let me emphasize that he is being corrected for *not sitting* rather than for going out to retrieve.

Many handlers send their dogs to retrieve after holding them for a second or two. They repeat this sequence for months until pup thinks he can retrieve on his own after one or two seconds. Dogs can count better than some people I know whether it be seconds on a watch or birds in a field. So, vary your cadence to send pup in each training session. Send him as soon as the bird hits the ground on one retrieve and make him wait ten seconds on the next. Pup will start to pay a lot more attention to you once he understands that he cannot have his bird until you say so.

FINISHED DOG

For those of you who have lofty goals of running your dog in events, there is one more thing your pup needs to learn. At most of these events, the judges will not allow you to send your dog to retrieve a bird until they release you by saying his number on the running list or the word "Dog". Practice this in your training sessions by having someone else say "Dog" or "Seven" or any other number before you send pup to retrieve. Over the years, I have seen a lot of dogs take off on the first sound they heard, so train those ears to listen for *his* name. Should he break, use the system described earlier to correct his misbehavior.

The process we have covered in this chapter is one of the easiest part of retriever training I experience. If you go slowly and let pup decide what pace he can accept with a wagging tail, this will be simple for you also.

FINISHED DOG

CHAPTER TWENTY-TWO

How does a dog improve his vision with a marking pattern?

One of my first good dogs was named Hank, and boy could that dog mark. After he matured, it was a rare day for Hank to be handled on a marked retrieve at a testing event. This was not the case for him as a young dog as he would hunt his heart out in the wrong place on a regular basis. When Hank turned about twenty-four months old, I was not fortunate enough to have a training group and relied on one friend, Tom Trimble, to help me keep Hank ready for events.

Tom and I would meet every morning at first light and throw birds for one another to prepare our dogs for NAHRA field tests. It was difficult to run the complex triples that we would see on Saturday mornings so we decided to do all single training and, it sure did work. Two marking patterns were thrown for the dogs at two different angles and distances form the running line. After the marks were picked up, the dogs were required to run one blind between the marking patterns and another outside one of the patterns. By doing this simple drill, we presented the dogs with virtually every concept that could be offered by a judge at an event or a flock of ducks sailing into a decoy rig. Oh yea, this worked so well that Hank went three and one-half years without failing a NAHRA or AKC test while maintained only by these drills.

Before we discuss what this magical marking pattern is and how it works, let's think about what a dog sees when looking at marks. The next time you are out training with your group, sit down on the ground and take a look at what your pup is processing when the birds go up. When you do this, it is evident that pup is working primarily in a two dimensional plain. First, he sees things fall at an angle on the horizon. This angle is formed by the position that you place pup in before the marks fall and is often defined by objects, terrain or cover in the field. These serve as markers to help keep pup on line when he is running out to the marks.

The second factor in marking is depth perception and, in my opinion, this is the most difficult skill for a dog to master. Short, long and in between marks can look very similar depending on the size of the bird or bumper when you take pup's view of the situation. The markers we discussed earlier are more important for depth acuity than angle precision.

If you believe what I have just said, then we can train or condition our dog's eyes to mark better by throwing marks in a way that forces him to focus on angle and depth in the field or pond. The marking pattern does this by constantly changing angle and depth with each retrieve. So, let's take a look at the marking pattern and how it works.

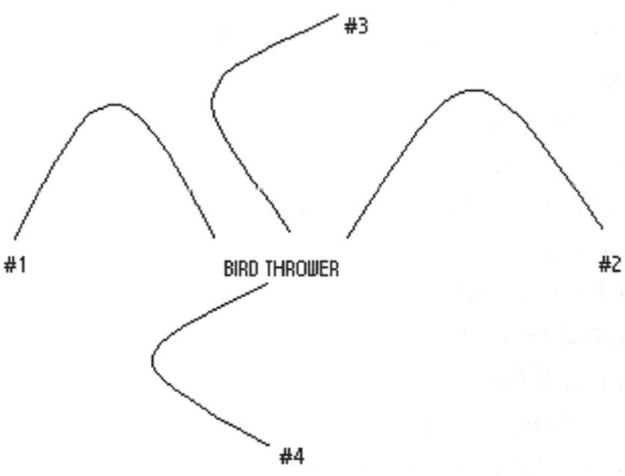

The thrower is to toss four single marked retrieves for pup from the same location. With the thrower facing you and pup, he tosses the first bird at a 90-degree angle to the left. This offers pup one angle on the horizon that will not be repeated. The next bird is thrown at a 90-degree angle to the right. It is the same distance from the running line but offers a totally different angle from the first mark. For those of you training for events, this is a simple way to prepare pup for those pain in the neck flower pot marks that always beg your dog to switch his hunt from one area of a fall to another. One left, one right, this is pretty simple.

Now the complexity begins as we work on pup's depth perception. The third mark is thrown straight back away from the bird station and away from pup. This requires pup to run past the bird station and maintain his focus as he passes between the previous marks. Pup is now required to run a new fine angle between two earlier angles and increase his distance. The last mark is thrown straight in directly toward pup. Now, pup is running the same angle but at a completely different distance. Right, left, back, front, now that is not so simple.

I like to throw this pattern for young dogs as soon as they have become technically sound with their transition from yard work to fieldwork. Pup must learn how to properly run the pattern first. This is best done in an open field with little cover or terrain changes. At first, the distances should be kept at a moderate length. Initial work demands that pup be successful. In the past, I have run this drill on golf course type areas for dogs that are struggling with the concept.

We have taken a look at these marks from our perspective, so now let's view them through pup's eyes. The left and right hand marks are fairly simple to most dogs. The birds are the same distance away as the bird station and the line to them is relatively uncluttered by previous retrieves. This is a great time to use pup's position at heel for alignment before the mark is thrown. With repetition, he will trust you and your direction on marks.

The mark thrown straight back can be very confusing for a young dog. He is asked to push past two previous marks while running directly between them. At the same time, he must negotiate the bird station, bird thrower and all the smells that go along with that spot. It is very common for pup to hang up around the station until he learns the routine, so be patient and have the bird thrower help him when necessary.

The final mark coming straight in causes my dogs more problems than all the rest combined. Pup has already gone deep three times and his depth gauge is set for long, long and longer. It is difficult for any dog to remain focused on short marks after "his lungs are full of air". Distance fixation occurs with pups when we start tossing fun bumpers and continues until we change the look by moving our bird throwers around. Pup has just finished running the same line at a much longer distance. If he has any heart and drive, he will want to push deep past the short bird. I start all new dogs on the marking pattern by having this mark in an open area void of cover. As pup's abilities grow, add a little more cover.

Once the pattern has been learned, it is time to move to different areas and repeat the routine. When pup becomes precise on each of the marks, place any hazard you are likely to encounter between pup and the bird station. He already knows the pattern, now he must negotiate the distractions and remain focused on the retrieve. Ground cover, terrain change, wind and lighting conditions all offer pup problems until he has become conditioned to work through them by repetition.

There is another consideration that must be discussed when throwing any mark for a dog. What does the background behind the bird thrower look like? Get down at pup's level and see how visible the marks are to your eye. How clear is the bird thrower? Can you see the bird as it leaves the thrower's hand? Does the bird disappear against a bright sky or blend into the trees 200 yards away? Are there hazards that prevent pup from seeing the bird all the way to the ground? Did the thrower use enough arc or was the throw flat? Have each of these questions in pup's favor when you set up a marking pattern. Most importantly, do not forget that you are training pup and not testing him. If pup has a hard time seeing the mark then how can he learn the concept? ***The most important point in any marking session is how clearly pup can see the marks.***

There are some problems that can arise while running a marking pattern and you need to be prepared to react to them when they occur. Throwing four marks from the same station creates a very tight picture to pup. Separation between the marks may only be twenty yards and with the bird station being 150 yards from our point of origin, twenty yards is not much. So, there is a great temptation for pup to switch his hunt from the area where his bird is waiting to another area where he may have already found a prize. I have tried various methods suggested to me over the years to correct a dog when he leaves the intended area for a forbidden spot. After all the experimenting, I have settled on letting pup continue to hunt until he finds the bird of his own accord or becomes totally confused. Confusion is defined by: leaving the area of the marking pattern and hunting a great distance away or trying to return to the handler. Pup does not believe that the bird is in the original area and has left it for greener pastures. Your bird thrower needs to help him find the mark using the methods previously discussed when this happens.

I am sure there are some of you wondering why I would allow a dog to go back to an old fall and hunt. This is considered a serious and failing fault in most every event. Remember, we are training and not testing in our day-to-day routines. It does not bother me in the least if a pup decides to check an area where he has already picked up a bird. Actually, it tells me that he has a pretty good memory. My theory on allowing a dog to "switch" is that he will never be rewarded for his misbehavior. He can hunt that area for as long as he desires but there will not be a bird there for him. He is failing himself by remaining there and the only way he can gain his reward, the bird, is by hunting away from that area. With time and repetition, confidence will come and with confidence comes precise marking. Be patient, let pup learn what failure is like and how fruitless going back to an old fall can be. He will get over this hurdle and if he does it on his own, we will all be better for it.

Another theory floating around is that we should not repeat marks if pup fails to perform properly. It is thought that repeating marks will encourage a dog to "switch" later on because he has been allowed in training to return to an old area and he is being rewarded for that behavior because there is a bird in the area. I have repeated marks with virtually every dog that I have trained and it is rare that any of them have a switching problem.

Routinely repeating marks is not a good idea. You must have a good reason to run the same mark multiple times in the same session. When we are working on concepts, pup can become confused and lose his focus on his mark. That can lead to a big hunt out of the area where the bird is located. Repeating that mark immediately will help pup learn that the hazards of the concept you are schooling are not that confusing, and he will likely push through them on his second chance. I do this with almost all of the young dogs until cover, terrain, angle water entries and any other hazard disappears from pup's vision. We want pup to no longer see the hazards. His entire focus should be on the spot where his bird is located and that comes with confidence, which is the result of repeated training on the concept.

There is another situation where I like to repeat a mark for pup. We have spoken of the importance of pup's confidence in himself and how that relates to his ability to mark. Dogs learn very quickly that they are in control while running marks and later they will learn that we are in control on blinds. As we start to assert more control during the handling program, many dogs rebel. A form of this rebellion that I routinely see is a lack of focus during marks. It can manifest itself in a couple of different forms.

Some dogs will continually swing their heads from side to side as the bird thrower attempts to gain pup's focus while throwing the bird. This dog is trying to control his situation by saying I am not going to look at the mark. If I do not look at the mark then maybe I will not have to go pick it up when you tell me to. This is a classic way for a dog to challenge the alpha position. It has nothing to do with his desire to retrieve but simple a test of who is in control. In this situation, I repeat the mark until pup's head swinging stops.

Head swinging is not that common but wandering around during the hunt for a mark is very normal for many dogs. They will go for the retrieve in a mad dash and take a quick turn flaring away from the mark hunting everywhere but the location of the bird. I cannot fathom how many times I have seen this happen. Once again, it has nothing to do with pup's desire to retrieve. This is solely a challenge of control. Pup is saying that he will pick up the bird but only when he is ready. When a dog displays this action, I let him hunt and hunt and hunt. I have been known to get a drink out of the cooler and pull up a chair until pup finally gives up and goes to the bird. Seldom do these dogs leave the area. They will run hard and put on a great act while they hunt the same area repeatedly. It may take thirty seconds or five minutes before they finally give up and retrieve their bird. The important thing is that pup resolve this himself. I have unsuccessfully attempted to force dogs into the area with various forms of pressure. This led to a loss of attitude and nothing more. Repeating the same mark until pup runs straight to the bird is a great fix for this problem. If he tries to refuse your control, he has to run and run but you still get your way when he finally retrieves the bird. Eventually with time and repetition, he will accept your alpha position again by taking those direct lines we all like to see.

We have talked of many things that will happen very quickly in this chapter. But, let's not forget what pup has learned before this chapter. Make sure you keep pup's skills intact as you are running the marking pattern. Do not allow him to slide in his mechanical ability to remain obedient, fetch on command, hold a bird and deliver it properly. Maintain the same standards you established in your previous training and never compromise your position as pup's alpha and before long you will have a dog that can mark as well as any Field Champion.

CHAPTER TWENTY-THREE

How does Pup learn basic handling skills?

Each year I attend an outdoor show in Charleston, South Carolina. The Southeastern Wildlife Exposition is a great venue for promoting my training ideas through videos, writings and demonstrations. I normally perform a couple of retriever demonstrations each day, using Scoop as the featured performer. He is a lot of fun and always attracts a large audience. Nobody cares about me. They just want to see Scoop, as it should be. As I proceed with the demonstration to a blind retrieve or two, the crowd always stirs when Scoop stops on a whistle and takes a cast in a new direction. Most novice dog people, myself included at one time, are amazed when a dog answers a whistle and takes a cast. It can be poetry in motion when the communication between dog and handler is clear.

Before we begin our discussion on how dogs learn to handle, let's define what Pup must do and why he would want to do it. Blind retrieves consist of a few basic skills. People try to make this a complex process when it is actually very simple. Pup must leave our side and go in a direction that we have "pointed" him. Next, he is required to stop and face us when hears our whistle. Then he must take a new direction from us by following the angle of our arm. Finally, Pup must pick up a bird and deliver it back to us. Sounds pretty simple, doesn't it?

If it is so simple, why do so many people have trouble when training their dog to handle? One of two things is normally the cause. Either they have a beta relationship with their dog, or Pup does not have the necessary basics to start a handling program. Before we can begin any handling drills, Pup must have finished his force fetch program, be marking well at distances that meet your requirements, and be very steady.

Even if the all of the above skills are in place, some dogs fail to handle well initially because of the relationship they display with their handler. Pup feels like he is the boss and still believes he is alpha. An alpha dog will not handle well until the handler becomes alpha and Pup accepts his role as beta. Notice I said ***accepts***. This is a very important concept, because, during the handling drills, Pup goes to retrieve because we tell him to go. There is no chase involved. The bumpers are down on the ground when we start and Pup goes to retrieve on blind faith in us. He must believe that there is always something there for him and, if he follows our direction, there must be a bird or bumper waiting for Pup. Eventually, Pup will go enthusiastically because he believes or has confidence in us. If we do our job correctly, he will know that we never lied to him because a bird or bumper will always be Pup's reward for following our lead, just as before. This sounds a lot like our previous lessons. In our marking drills, Pup developed confidence in himself. With our handling drills, he will now become confident in us.

Where is the starting point in training a dog to handle? There are a few opinions on this topic but I choose to begin with my favorite tool, the fun bumper. Place a pile of bumpers about twenty-five yards away and then toss a few fun bumpers into the pile for Pup to retrieve. This identifies the pile as a good place for Pup and a spot that holds a reward for him. After his momentum is good and both of you are comfortable, sit Pup with your whistle, *tweet,* and walk away so that Pup is seated directly between you and the pile of bumpers. We are now going to start a casting drill with Pup. Take two steps to your right, and raise your right hand directly over your head as you toss another fun bumper to the pile with *Hup, hup, hup.* Pup should turn to his left and run eagerly to the pile retrieving a bumper. Meet him back at the original spot to receive the bumper, seating him with your whistle when he comes to the proper heel position. Repeat this until Pup is rabid over his new drill.

A couple of undesirable things can occur while you are doing this simple first step. Pup may decide not to remain seated, but walk to you when you move away from him. If this happens, reinforce your *tweet* by taking Pup back to the spot and not proceeding until Pup accepts that he must sit away from you and await his next direction. Do not toss his fun bumper until he demonstrates that he can remain under control. His reward for this act will be the fun bumper.

Another problem I have seen occurs when Pup comes back to you instead of going for the retrieve. This is usually the result of too much pressure in forcing a dog to heel. When Pup feels pressure, he runs to your heel position in an effort to escape the pressure. For this problem, be persistent and take him back to the original spot. Use a little more tone in your voice to instruct Pup that you are not happy with him coming to you. If you are using an e-collar, use your *tweet-nick-tweet* to correct his wrong actions by seating him back at spot between you and the bumper pile. Keep tossing fun bumpers until he is happily moving to the bumper pile instead of coming back to you. Meet Pup back at the original casting spot, and do lots of repetitions, making sure that Pup always turns to his right and goes directly to the bumper pile.

A very common distraction that happens with virtually every dog is shopping when they get to the bumper pile. They search through the pile of bumpers until they find the one bumper that was last thrown. This used to bother me a great deal and was a sure fire way to be corrected. My views on shopping have changed recently, and now I let them continue searching through the pile until they find their prize. It is a self-limiting problem. Eventually, Pup will pick up the first available bumper, and this shopping mentality has yet to cause any of our dog's problems. As before, they accept this when they are ready. Some folks will electrically fetch Pup to the pile at this point. Be patient—that will come later, this needs to be fun now.

Okay, we have overcome the problems, and Pup is spinning enthusiastically to his right each time we toss a bumper and raise our right hand. Now, it is time to repeat the process to the left. Seat Pup between you and the bumper pile, move away from him, take a few steps to your left and start tossing fun bumpers from this side. Use your left hand now instead of your right. Pup should pick this up very quickly. One problem that can occur is for Pup to spin to his left instead of his right. If this occurs, correct him with *NO!*, call Pup back to the original spot, and repeat the process after taking a few more steps to your left.

Continue the repetitions from both sides until Pup will eagerly spin left or right, depending on which hand you use for casting. This is called "directional casting" and will be very useful in the future. Pup now knows the bumper pile is a good place that holds rewards for him. He also understands that your right hand turns him to his left and your left hand spins him to his right. Pup is comfortable sitting away from you and taking a new direction. This is a great start.

Our next step is having Pup remain steady when we toss a bumper back to the pile. Sit Pup at the starting spot, and command him to sit with a *tweet,* then, toss a bumper to the pile. If Pup moves, call him back and repeat the process until he remains seated. Pup should be focused on you but he may decide to look at the bumper pile. If this happens, shake a bumper in your hand or rattle your whistles to get his attention. When he is looking at you, raise the correct arm directly over your head and cast him back with *fetch.* Repeat this to the left and right as before, until you have a precise mechanical response. When Pup is moving well, start commanding *fetch-back* to send him. Later leave off the *fetch* and just use *back.* Be patient if Pup hesitates on the word change until he is comfortable with either word.

The above process may take three days or two weeks, depending on the dog. Please do not get into a timetable when training Pup to handle. This is a tough mental procedure and we must go at his pace. I see a lot of attitude lost when people attempt to force Pup through these drills. I encourage you not to go there.

After Pup is moving well and driving back to the pile, stop tossing a bumper before you send him. If we did our homework, Pup should understand what we are asking him to do and drive back to the pile when we command *back*, spinning left or right, depending on which arm we use. Each time we continue to meet Pup at the original spot for delivery and blow a *tweet* on our whistle when he comes to the correct heel position. Back up moving away from Pup and start to create some distance between the two of you. When he is comfortable with this, move Pup's casting spot further from the bumper pile, requiring him to cover more distance when he is cast.

You may be twenty-five yards from Pup and he may be twenty-five yards from the bumper pile at this point. If he is moving well, we will start to add a few distractions by tossing a bumper over Pup's head to the bumper pile as Pup returns with his retrieve. This is the beginning of distraction training. Should Pup decide to switch bumpers by dropping the one in his mouth and going for the one you tossed, stop him with *No* command him to pick up the proper bumper with *fetch.* Repeat this until Pup no longer acknowledges the bumper as it sails over his head.

A problem that occurs in casting dogs is the failure to go when cast. This is called "no-go" and is a blatant refusal to do as commanded. I see this in many dogs after they have been in the casting routine for a few days. They begin to realize that I am controlling all of their actions. To challenge my alpha position, they choose to no-go instead of following my command to retrieve. In their words, "I am not going to do what you tell me, old man." This is a bad day for most dogs, because we now must resolve the alpha-beta relationship or quit training.

Forcing to the pile has been done by almost every trainer and is the least desirable thing I do with dogs. They choose to refuse our command to retrieve and we have to use the communication skills already in place to send them on. For the non-collar dog, this can be a problem. We must go back to toe pressure, in an effort to force Pup to retrieve on command. This can be done by tapping his toe with your boot or attaching a longer toe hitch, like the one we used during walking fetch. Use the walking fetch drill while picking up all of the bumpers at the pile until Pup gets the idea that he must go when commanded. Stay with this drill until Pup no longer challenges your position. This may take one day or one week.

For the e-collar dog, go back to your walking electric fetch drill and repeat that process while sending Pup to the pile of bumpers. *Fetch-nick-fetch* should be used until Pup is freely moving to the pile and returning to your side with the bumpers. After *fetch-nick-fetch,* substitute *back-nick-back* so Pup will understand that *back* and *fetch* mean the same thing.

There are some that use continuous stimulation at this point instead of the momentary nicks. For some dogs, I have successfully done this. If you choose this route, be very careful of your intensity. Momentary nicks and continuous burns at the same level may not produce the same results. Use the lowest level that will move Pup to the bumper pile without vocalizations. It is probably a good idea to leash Pup during this process to prevent him from attempting to bolt away from you. We have always preached to never add pressure, mental or physical, to a dog that is feeling pressure. You may need to violate that rule in this process at some point. Let Pup dictate the pace, duration and intensity. Once the no-goes are resolved, they seldom, if ever, return. Pup has accepted that he is to go when commanded.

Now, it is time to add the *over* casts and this is done in the same manner as the *back* casts. These will be 90-degree casts to the left and right, while your *backs* are 180-degree casts straight back. Place a pile of bumpers directly to Pup's left and right. Seat Pup at his original place, and toss a bumper to either his left or right into the bumper pile. Use the appropriate arm to cast Pup *over* to the pile. Once the pile is identified, he should cast easily back to the pile on successive casts. Repeat this until he is moving well, then, repeat everything on the other side. If all went well in the *back* casting, the *overs* will be easy. Continue rotating your casts from right *back,* to left *over,* to right *over,* to left *back*, until Pup can perform them flawlessly. Always meet Pup at the same point to receive his delivery of the bumper. Also, blow the whistle every time he comes to the heel position for delivery.

This looks a lot like a baseball field where we stand at home plate, Pup is on the pitcher's mound, bumpers are at first, second and third bases. We choose which base he goes to retrieve with our arm and verbal casts. Pup knows three spots that hold bumpers for him. He gets to pick one up, but only the one we allow, and only in the direction we cast. With enough repetition, Pup will soon learn to follow our lead and each time he follows our lead, he gets something he wants. We never lie to him, and he learns to trust our direction. That's progress.

Pup has also learned something that will be very useful later—to sit on a whistle at a certain spot in the field. We will get back to that shortly.

Some programs promote starting with *over* casting first, and then proceeding to the *back* casts. I used to do this, but all of those dogs struggled when we got to the *backs.* In my opinion, the dogs were turning to their left or right and looking directly at the *over* piles, wanting to go to them instead of back where we were casting them. This resulted in conditioned confusion. Start with your *backs*, and then add the *overs*. The picture is clearer in Pup's eyes.

For those of you using the e-collar, now is the time to force the *back* and *over* casts. Use the same techniques that were successful when forcing to the pile. *Back-nick-back* and *over-nick-over* should be done every third or fourth cast depending on Pup's response for a couple of days to reinforce the casting issue. Be especially attentive of Pup's attitude. If he shows any signs of momentum loss, back off quickly. Start tossing fun bumpers to revive Pup and demonstrate to him that the area is no problem.

During all of this you should continue to throw marked retrieves for your dog. I know this brings up debate among other training programs, but, in my opinion, this is very important. It keeps Pup happy in his daily work and prevents any loss of confidence in his ability to mark. I have seen some dogs completely lose their ability to find marks when going through the handling program. They become so confident in their handler that they lose their confidence in themselves. These dogs begin to pop and ask the handler for direction when they do not find their marks. For the rest of Pup's life, one of our primary jobs will be balancing Pup's confidence in himself and in us. But, we are off to a great start.

CHAPTER TWENTY-FOUR

What is the easiest way for Pup to learn to whistle-stop?

I receive calls from people every week wondering how we train dogs to stop on a whistle when they are moving away from us. This seems to amaze people more than any other skill dogs learn. Often, they ask if they can borrow one of my e-collars so they can *teach* their dog to stop when they blow the whistle. That is usually the end of our conversation. First, I do not loan e-collars to people that do not know how to operate them, and, most importantly, there are no quick fixes when it comes to training a dog to remotely stop on a whistle.

We spoke of training Pup to voice and whistle commands from the beginning. If you have done your homework before now, having him stop on a whistle while he is running away from you will be a piece of cake. Before asking Pup to whistle-stop in the field for the first time, it is a good idea to do some obedience routines using only the whistle. Vary the routine so you do not become predictable. Pay close attention to Pup's attitude while you are doing this drill and look for the conditioned responses. Be especially tuned in to his swallow response. When he accepts the whistle, he will swallow when he sits. Continue to repeat the obedience drills if Pup is not precise on his stops and do not move into the field until he is precise and happy with this form of command.

So, now that we have a Pup that is sitting well on the whistle around the yard, where do we begin our whistle-stop in the field? I go to the casting pattern where we just finished working. Pup has been conditioned to sit at the pitcher's mound position through repeated work while casting. Not only is he conditioned to perform the skill, but also at this spot. Start here and build by adding distance for the rest of Pup's life.

Begin by going back to the casting field. You and Pup start at the home plate position. Toss a bumper to the *back* pile and send Pup for the retrieve. Repeat this routine a time or two until he is moving well. Send him again and this time, blow your whistle as he approaches the pitcher's mound. I will bet you my best duck call that Pup will stop and face you the first time. After he sits, tell him what a good dog he is and cast him to any of the piles for the retrieve. Pour the praise on when he returns with the bumper. That's one. Thousands more are ahead of us before we can venture into the field. As the conditioning and precision grow, we will move to different areas, but not until then.

We have described a rosy picture. What happens if Pup decides not to be an ideal student? I have seen dogs stop, then walk back to me. Others have blatantly refused to answer the whistle. Do not continue to blow your whistle in hopes of Pup stopping at some time. He gets one chance to do this correctly before we correct him. Still others will stop, look at me, and then go on to the pile on their own. None of these are acceptable and must be corrected instantly by using the same method.

If you are training without an e-collar and Pup refuses to stop on your whistle, stop him with a verbal *No* using an angry tone. Run to the pitcher's mound, and call Pup back to you. When he comes to heel, blow your whistle. After he sits, blow it again and command *Sit*. Go back to home plate, and cast Pup to the desired bumper pile. Repeat the scenario until Pup is doing it properly. Be very careful about how many times you stop Pup with your whistle, and never stop him twice in a row. This can lead to popping or Pup stopping himself without you blowing a whistle. Send him all the way to the second base pile every other time without stopping him to prevent a popping mentality from developing.

For those of you using an e-collar, the correction procedure is the same. The only difference is when you run out and sit Pup with your whistle. The e-collar trainer will use a *tweet-nick-tweet*. You still need to go out to the spot and correct Pup initially. Now, I hope you can see the importance of having Pup be able to accept his e-collar correction without moving around. Imagine how difficult this scene would be with Pup jumping around, due to over stimulation. So, when you begin stopping

FINISHED DOG

Pup in the field, make sure you wear your tennis shoes that day. You might need them, especially if you did not do your homework. Of all the things I train dogs to do, this is the easiest. I attribute that to preparation. Make sure Pup is a good Boy Scout with lots of preparation before you ask him to perform this skill.

CHAPTER TWENTY-FIVE

What is Single-T?

Now, we are getting into the meat of our handling drills, and there are other bases to cover even if you think Pup has it all figured out. Single-T is a drill that ties all the conditioned responses of casting from our side, whistle-stop, and *back* and *over* casting. Essentially, we are running very short blinds to three spots. Pup knows that there is a reward for him at each of these spots, and he should be eager to go there. Many trainers today call this drill "Mini-T." Richard Wolters called it "baseball" in his books. We will take what the old man taught us and add a few twists, so let's go.

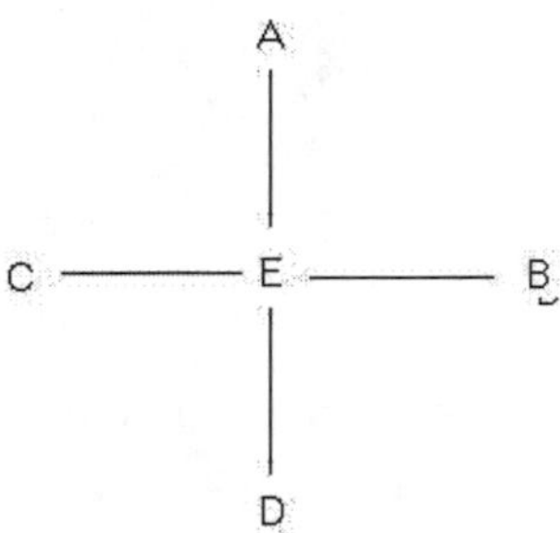

Go back to your casting field, and place a pile of bumpers at second base (A), first base (B), and third base (C). You and Pup go to home plate (D). Toss a bumper to A, and cast Pup with a hand in front of his face and a verbal *back*. Repeat this until Pup is moving well from D to A and happily retrieving his bumpers. Now, send him from D, whistle-stop him at E and give him a *back* cast using the proper hand to A. Make sure Pup turns the correct way. If you get a whistle refusal (failure to stop when whistle is blown), correct with *No-tweet* (non e-collar) or *NO-tweet-nick-tweet* (e-collar), as we described in the last chapter.

Our next cast will be all the way from D to A without stopping. Pour the praise on as he returns to help the attitude. The following cast will be from D to E, with a whistle-stop and an *over* cast to C. After Pup returns, send Pup from D to A again. Now we are going to add some flavor. Send Pup from D to a spot between E and A, with a whistle-stop. This is a new spot for Pup to answer our whistle, so be prepared if he does not. When you get him seated, call him back to E with a *tweet-tweet* and whistle-stop at E. Then, cast him to B with an *over.* When he returns, send him from D to A again. Next, send Pup from D to a spot between D and E, with a whistle-stop. Cast him *back*, making sure Pup takes the correct directional *back* (left or right hand) all the way to A. Finish by sending him from D to A.

FINISHED DOG

This is a complex little drill in Pup's mind. He goes out and back and over and back out. He must continually follow our lead. But, each time that he accepts our direction, he is rewarded with a bumper. This should be repeated for a period of weeks or months until you have a precise handling Pup with lots of momentum. When finished, Pup will have all the technical skills necessary to run blind retrieves, but not the experience. That will come with a few more drills.

While running Single-T, keep throwing marks for Pup. That will keep his eyes sharp and his attitude upbeat. If things get too sour, shoot him a live bird or two. I cannot emphasize keeping an eye on Pup's attitude enough during this phase of his training. I see more loss of momentum and attitude at this point than all of the others put together. I believe this is the result of continually being told to retrieve without having any chase involved in the game. Pup gets a prize when he picks up a bumper, but it may take a while for some Pups to realize this. Don't be afraid to mix a fun bumper into the routine if you see some loss of attitude. Pup will like you for it.

FINISHED DOG

CHAPTER TWENTY-SIX

How do we correct Pup's wrong casts?

Occasionally, our star students decide to take their own path and go their own way when we are handling them. We all have seen this at events where the judges have set up a maze of hazards for Pup to travel through. Or, it could be in the dove field, duck marsh or goose pit. We need Pup to go one way when he is committed to go another. Why would a dog decide he knows where to go and we don't? I believe it relates to how much conditioning has been done in the Single-T pattern field and Pup's alpha/beta relationship to his handler.

In the Single-T pattern field, Pup may choose to go left when you try to cast him right. Or, he may be digging hard on a right over even though your arm and voice are casting him back. What is on his mind to cause these blatant refusals? In the beginning of our handling program, we need to expect refusals out of Pup and actually welcome them. Yes, he needs to learn what pleases. The real value in a dog that handles well comes when he displays how he can recover from a mistake and continue his work with confidence in us. In the ideal world of training, we would not allow Pup to make those mistakes. However, I hate to break it to you, but no one lives in an ideal world. Both you and Pup are going to make plenty of mistakes, so let's figure out how to correct his errors and learn from this situation.

Cast refusals are going to happen, and we need a system to comfortably correct Pup when he makes mistakes. I learned of the attrition system of correction many years ago and have been fiddling with it over the years, in an effort to simplify it for Pups and handlers. In this system, we will continually call Pup back to the spot where he made his mistake and repeat the correct cast until he takes it. For example, if we want to cast Pup from E to B in the Single-T drill and he goes to A instead, use attrition to correct his wrong casts.

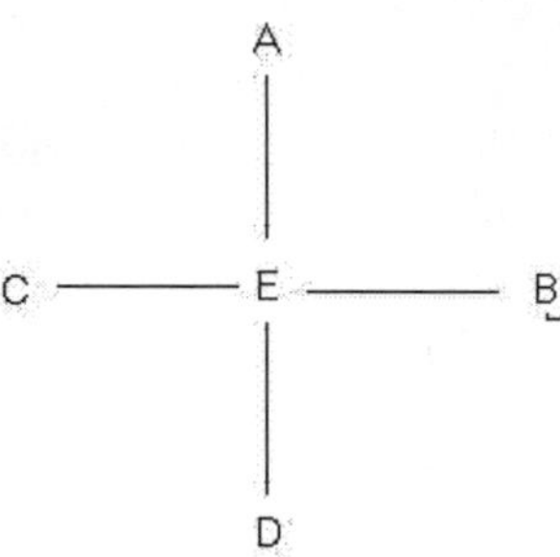

As he goes for A, stop him with your whistle, call him back to E, seat him with your whistle and repeat the cast to B. If he continues to go for A, continue to call him back to E, seat him with your whistle and repeat the cast to B. It is a matter of who is more earnest, and I suggest that you never lose that battle. You simply wear Pup down with whistle-stops and check in whistles until he says, "Okay, I'll do it."

This scenario sounds a great deal like the rest of our training. You are not forcing him to go to B. You simply are not allowing him to go anywhere but B. He accepts your cast when he is ready. That is a training concept he learned from day one in our program. It will remain in place for the rest of Pup's life. Be consistent as he learns the system, and you will have a dog that handles like a Ferrari.

I use attrition a great deal as Pup learns the Single-T and Double-T drills. He is going to become confused. Adding physical pressure to his confusion will definitely result in loss of momentum and/or attitude. He has a limited amount of both of these to spare. In his early training, Pup is not well conditioned. We must be patient until he knows the rules and has demonstrated that to us for an extended period of time. Doing something correctly two or three times does not constitute mastering the drill.

For argument's sake, let's say you are casting Pup *over* and he goes *back*. You are a good trainer and quickly check him back in, instituting the attrition system of correction. After about five minutes of attrition, Pup still believes he is correct and goes *back.* How do we get out of this mess? First, keep your cool. I have lost my focus a time or two when this happened, and I hope you can learn from my experience. Resist the temptation to pound him —you will not like yourself when you finish, and Pup will think a lot less of you also.

For this very situation, I started keeping a bumper in my back pocket when running any casting drill or new blind with an inexperienced dog. If I have tried attrition until I am satisfied that Pup is not going to accept my cast, I go to plan B (for BUMPER). Call Pup back to the spot where he continually took the wrong cast and seat him. Take the bumper from your back pocket, and toss it to the spot where Pup should have gone. Then, cast him to that spot. He will fly to the bumper. The pressure is now off both of you. Trainer and dog got out of this uncomfortable situation with both of their heads up. Now, repeat the routine. I bet you a steak dinner he will take the cast the first time you give it. Some trainers may view this as giving in to the dog and not maintaining the alpha position. Let them train their dogs. You train yours. Pup will tell you with his swallows and tail wags who is right. Pay attention to what he is saying.

You notice that I have not mentioned using the e-collar up to this point. That was done for a reason. I want to emphasize the use of attrition to the nth degree before applying physical pressure to our student. Most e-collar people become push button trainers to some degree. They push the transmitter button in an effort to gain a correct response from Pup. With proper conditioning, this works very well. But please remember, Pup is learning, and his ego is very fragile now. Because of this, I do not use my e-collar to correct cast refusals until we have finished running the entire Double-T drill. At that time, I am confident that Pup knows how to run the drill and has been well conditioned to perform those skills in that area.

While we are here, let's go ahead and talk about correcting Pup's wrong casts using an e-collar. The most accepted system I have seen for doing this involves using indirect pressure. That means that we are going to correct Pup for taking an incorrect cast by seating him with the whistle, *nicking* him with the e-collar, calling Pup back to spot where he took the wrong cast, reseating him with the whistle and repeating the original cast. Once again, I hope you can see how important it is for Pup to be able to remain seated and under total control while being stimulated. A good collar-conditioning program is a must before you correct Pup in the field for his mistakes.

Think for a moment about what happened to Pup in the last paragraph and why he would want to take our cast the second time around. He went his way and was corrected for going there. The stimulation forms a wall *at that spot* to him and he is not likely to venture into the wall again. He may choose to go a direction other than our cast again, especially if he is challenging your alpha role. But, it is very unlikely that he will go back to the spot where you corrected him. Keep building walls with *nicks* and attrition until he takes the correct cast.

I have a few rules about correction. First, Pup must not be corrected unless you are certain he has been conditioned (not merely shown) to perform the skill you are commanding. Next, Pup must be conditioned to perform the skill in the arena in which you are training. If you are running field blinds for the first time, he is not conditioned to perform in that arena. That comes with experience and repetition. Finally, never apply physical pressure (stimulation with the e-collar) until you have given Pup multiple chances to do the job correctly. In other words, try attrition before using indirect pressure with your e-collar.

Something exciting happens when you consistently use this approach. Pup learns that if he does not take your cast after your first attempt at attrition, e-collar stimulation follows. After enough repetitions in this system, your use of attrition will mean the same thing as e-collar stimulation to Pup. Mr. Pavlov described this as substitution. I use it at field tests all the time and it works great. I check Pup in one step and give him the cast I need. In his mind, I *nicked* him with the collar, and he will take my next cast.

We have spoken of cast refusals in the field but what about no-goes? To me these are cast refusals also. Some no goes occur in the field when Pup hangs up and refuses to move when cast. Others occur at heel when you attempt to send Pup on his initial line to the blind. In both cases, you want to get Pup moving as quickly as possible. For the dog at heel, I step forward with a *heel* command, and then send Pup again. If he still refuses, I resort back to the e-collar with a *heel-nick-heel*, and then send him with a forceful verbal *back*.

Failure to cast in the field drives me nuts. Pup just sits there, thinking he is safe, instead of moving when commanded. This guy is usually feeling mental pressure, and that needs to be relieved. Sometimes a simple check in whistle will get Pup moving, and that may be all that is needed to jump start him. Other times, you might have to resort to *cast-nick-cast.* To be safe, make sure you have a bumper in your back pocket, and do not forget plan B.

A lot has happened in this chapter. We have built a system of communication that is awesome. Pup understands what we want, because a consistent system is in place. He readily accepts our lead due to repetition and conditioning. We can add to the communication with an e-collar as needed and have Pup comfortable with his situation. And finally, this can be transferred to any new arena at a later time. Many trainers stop here because they feel these are all the skills that Pup needs. Let's not do that—there are a few more tools we can put into his box that will add precision and confidence to his work.

FINISHED DOG

CHAPTER TWENTY-SEVEN

Why do we use a Double-T drill?

In the Single-T drill, a dog learns the technical skills necessary to run blind retrieves. Double-T takes the skills of Single-T and hones them to perfection with repetition. This is one of my favorite drills to watch a dog learn. They begin as a confused mess, constantly challenging the alpha position. In the end, they run confidently and are glad to take a cast in any direction. Dogs never see the world in the same light after completing Double-T.

I have seen Double-T patterns that are very long, 250-300 yards. This may be necessary for some programs, but I think we can accomplish all that is required and keep the distance around 100 yards. Extended distances can lead to exhaustion, especially during warm months, and some lack of attention that decreases Pup's precision. For that reason, my pattern field is 100 yards form H to A. The *over* legs (B, C, F and G) need to be far enough apart to prevent Pup from switching while he is running from F to A, but not so far as to lead to exhaustion. I set my B to C and F to G distances at 50 yards. Finally H to D and E to A are 25 yards leaving D to E at 50 yards. Set yours how you wish, but this seems to cover all the bases for me.

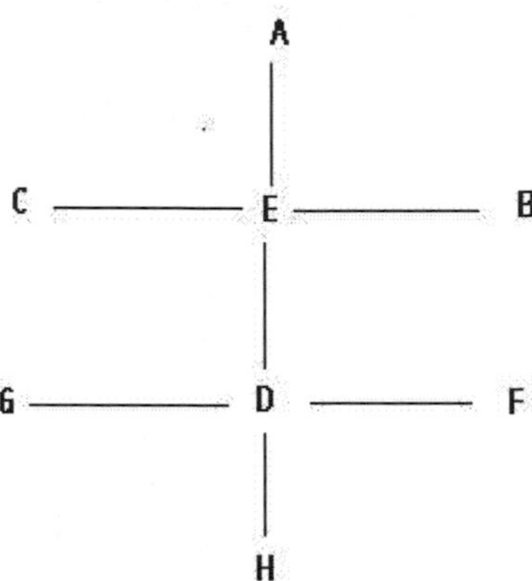

When you finished running Single-T, your position is between D and E. As Pup shows confidence and some knowledge of what you are asking, back up toward H slowly. Do not be surprised if Pup hesitates or loses a little momentum as you back up. He is on new ground and not quite sure if the same rules apply. Reassure him and continue with enough repetitions to gain Pup's confidence. Toss a fun bumper or two if Pup starts to fade.

When you have backed up to your D position, add another set of *over* legs (G and F) to form your Double-T. Pup should easily cast to them, but use attrition and keep plan B in your pocket just in case he becomes confused. After this is accomplished, back from D to H slowly. I have seen this take many days for some headstrong dogs. Currently, I am working with a young Lab named Wags. He is giving me grief from H to D. After he gets to D, Wags is a well-oiled machine. Our alpha/beta relationship is still being resolved, but I am seeing more swallow responses from him each day. We are headed in the right direction. Keep a close eye on your Pup's attitude and watch for the swallows—he will tell you when he accepts.

Pup now has five spots that hold a reward. There is a specific sequence to run Double-T. Each cast sets up the next cast as you begin to push and pull your dog around the pattern. Here is the sequence that I began using some years ago. Always begin by casting Pup from H to A without stopping. This will be repeated on every other send, in an effort to prevent popping. Repeat this "free run" any time you see Pup lose momentum or focus. We want our dogs to run hard on blind retrieves, and that begins with good momentum in our Double-T pattern.

After Pup returns from A to your side, line him up and send him to E, with a whistle-stop. When he gives you his full attention, put your arm out at a 90-degree angle and cast him to B, with an *over*. When he delivers this bumper, send him on another "free run" from H to A.

Our fourth send works on the attrition skills that we will use for the rest of Pup's life. Cast Pup from H to a spot about halfway between D and E, with a whistle-stop. When he is seated and focused on you, give him a *tweet-tweet* and call him back to D, whistle-stopping him at D. This is the process we will use when Pup gives us a cast refusal in the pattern field or training field. As Pup settles in at D, cast him *over* to G. He may have a tendency to lean toward F, because he took a right *over* on his last stop. We need Pup to follow our lead, and he learns this in Double-T. So, if Pup wants to go in one direction, cast him in the other. In a short period of time, Pup will become confident that you know where all of his rewards are located.

On the fifth send, Pup goes from H to A, with no stops. This is followed by the money sequence. Now we are going to find out to what degree Pup trusts us. The sixth send is very complex in Pup's mind. We cast him from H to D, with a whistle-stop. At D, we cast Pup straight *back*, making sure you use the correct arm and he turns the proper direction. The last time Pup was at D, he took an *over* now he must go *back*. Be prepared in case Pup tries to go *over* instead of *back*. When he takes his *back*, whistle-stop him again at E. As Pup focuses on you, cast him *over* to C. He will be inclined to go straight back toward A, so be prepared for this. Use attrition if he continues to push *back* instead of taking the *over*. In these few casts, we have scrambled Pup's brain. He wants to go in one direction but we continually control his actions by sending him in another. When a dog successfully completes this sequence, I feel pretty good about his future.

On Pup's seventh trip, he free spools from H to A. The eighth send goes from H to D, with a whistle-stop. From D, we cast Pup *over* to F. By now, Pup is starting to believe. Finish the drill by repeatedly casting Pup from H to A until his momentum is excellent.

Keep an upbeat tone with Pup throughout the drill, except when you are correcting him for whistle or cast refusals. Watch for acceptance of your correction with a swallow from Pup. He will tell you if you will pay attention. As he accepts your leadership role, a very strong trust forms between the two of you. In the future this confidence in each other will allow you to recover any bird in any location. Always reward Pup for his good work with a few fun bumpers from H to D after you finish this drill. He likes this, and you are thanking him for his efforts. Think of this as Pup's bonus check.

In the real world, Pup will make plenty of mistakes in the casting sequence we have described. Cast refusals, and even some whistle refusals, are going to happen. We have discussed how to correct them, but let's go a little deeper.

We are setting Pup up to give us cast refusals in an effort to gain the skills necessary for precise handling. He must understand that correction is not the end of the world, but merely a way of learning to trust us. So, be judicious with your corrections. A crushing *NO!* should only be used when you are positive that Pup knows what you want and is blatantly refusing to follow your lead. Many times I will walk toward Pup when he refuses my casts. This decreases the distance between us and intimidates Pup to a small degree. Quite often, that is all it takes to straighten him up. He thinks I might be crazy enough to come out there and correct him.

Anytime Pup is giving you grief with a cast refusal, analyze the problem. What is causing him to disobey your lead? Is there a hazard that has his attention? Did he receive a correction in the direction you want him to go? Is the wind blowing up a gale, and does he not want to put his nose into that wind? Can he smell the bumper pile at another station? Look at what is causing the problem in Pup's performance, and then use attrition, indirect e-collar pressure or a tossed bumper to get out of the situation with all parties looking good. Do not give in to Pup and put him up without gaining what you need. If it takes heeling him over to the spot, make sure you remain in the alpha position and gain what you have commanded Pup to do.

Whistle refusals are not very common when running Double-T. By now, they should be well conditioned, especially in this arena. However, they do occur and as before, we need to know why. Some dogs will "skip" a whistle in an effort to avoid being cast. Pup is thinking that if he does not stop on the whistle, then he will not have to follow our cast and, therefore, he is not beta to us. Dogs can and do reason this out. I have seen this many times following a correction. As with our cast refusals, figure out why Pup failed to stop on the whistle before you correct him. Was the wind blowing so hard that maybe he did not hear you? Probably not, but make sure you understand why the problem occurred before you attempt to fix it.

In any case, you must correct him quickly. Run Pup down if necessary, and take him back to the spot where he refused your whistle-stop. Seat him with the whistle, and correct using a verbal *SIT!* or *nick* with the e-collar if that is your method. Then, repeat the sequence to emphasize how you want Pup to perform. In reality, there are no excuses for whistle refusals, and they must be corrected quickly. Failing to do so will start a snowball rolling that may never be stopped.

Popping will most likely occur at some time during the drill. We continually whistle-stop Pup at the same spots, and he will learn that we like it when he sits there. This can lead to popping at D and E. To a large degree, we have caused this problem. If Pup demonstrates this to you, quickly cast him on with a simple arm motion. Add a stern verbal *back* cast if he displays this action in the future. Popping is the product of a lack of confidence. Pup has been conditioned to stop at certain spots and thinks he should sit instead of confidently carrying out the command to continue going until we stop him. Or, Pup is worried about going to an area, maybe because he was corrected there earlier. Pup is more confident while sitting than going. This is not good and should set sirens off in your head. Show Pup that you want him to move through the area by tossing fun bumpers or casting him. Relieve the pressure by whatever means and repeat the cast until Pup moves freely through the "pop" area. When a dog pops in Double-T, it is not uncommon for me to send him from H to A ten to fifteen times in a row for a period of days.

Double-T is run with Pup for about a month. It becomes very boring for both dog and handler, but persevere. We must condition responses very well if Pup is to follow our lead at long distances, and conditioning is the reward of repetition. Turn on the radio and listen to a few tunes if you get bored. Give Pup a fun bumper when he needs an attitude adjustment. Both handler and dog need a positive attitude while working on this drill, so make it fun. Tell Pup he is good with a touch on his shoulder and an upbeat tone of voice. Pup will like you for it, and you will like what he is doing.

Some people, myself included, mow paths in their Double-T pattern. This makes it easy for Pup to cast where we want him to go, since all animals instinctively choose the easiest path. I prefer to drive my wife's car on the road instead of through the trees in the woods. Think of the mowed paths as training wheels. Later you will take them away. Pup may choose to take the easy path in his later training, but, through attrition, we will correct his direction. Some trainers worry that this may become a big problem and encourage Pup to cheat and take the easy way out. If we stopped here, that would be true, but we still have a lot of ground to cover.

While running Double-T continue throwing marked retrieves for Pup. It will keep him and you in a good frame of mind. Double-T can lead to a great deal of correction causing Pup to lose some of his positive attitude. A few confidence marks or a shot flyer will improve any loss of attitude. It gives him a breather during the day where you can work on other important skills. Do you think you are ready to go run some blinds now? Not yet, we still have work to do.

FINISHED DOG

CHAPTER TWENTY-EIGHT

What is the importance of handling on the return?

By now, we have a dog that stops on a whistle and takes a relatively precise cast in the direction we desire. This is impressive and leads some people to hurry out to the field and run blind retrieves with Pup. If you conditioned Pup well enough, you can probably get by and head for the field. But there are a few more skills Pup needs, and handling while he is returning to us with a bumper in his mouth is one of them.

Pup's retrieving instinct has been nurtured to a level where he hurries back to us on a retrieve for several reasons. He is anticipating his next retrieve and wants to hurry back so the chase can begin again. Pup also knows that retrieving pleases us and pleasing us now pleases him. Finally, we have conditioned the heel position as a safe place for Pup to be. Heel has become a den-like spot for him.

As we are controlling Pup's actions at all times, he must learn to accept our control as he returns with a bumper in his mouth. For the reasons discussed above, Pup wants to hurry back to our side. We want to emphasize our alpha role on him by controlling when he can return to us. This solidifies the alpha/beta roles and continues to condition whistle-stop and casting skills. To me, this is the ultimate conditioning drill. All of his instincts tell him to do one thing, while we command him to do another. This requires total trust in you by Pup.

Unlike Double-T, there is no set drill or sequence when handling a dog on his return. The skills are learned in the Double-T pattern field. I generally ask Pup to stop and handle on his return after a "free run" cast from H to A. In other words, I do not handle on the way out and on the way back also. You can, but expect a great deal of loss in momentum. I may ask Pup to handle on his return on casts three and five during the Double-T sequence.

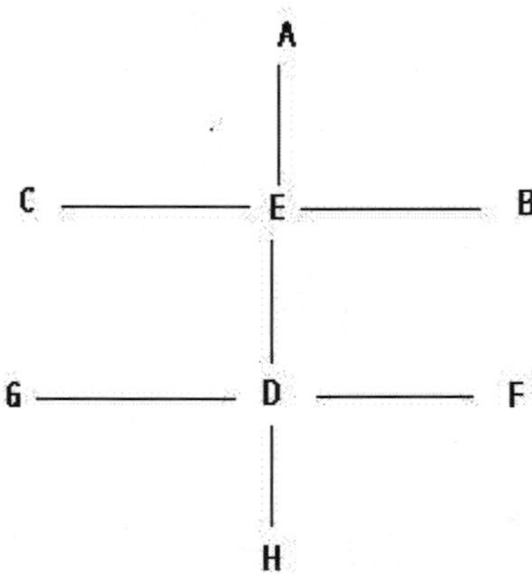

This is a great way to work on whistle-stop and casting skills when a dog is demonstrating popping tendencies.

Send him from H to A every time, and work on the handling skills only as he returns. This builds momentum and allows the continuance of conditioning whistle-stop and casting.

There a few things that Pup will do when you begin to handle him on his return. First, he may refuse to stop in an attempt to hurry back to your side. For this, you must hustle out to him and correct the whistle refusal using the methods we discussed earlier. Make sure you take him to the exact spot where he refused your whistle when you make the correction. Verbal correction or e-collar, it is your choice. Watch for his acceptance. It is a little harder for him to swallow when he has a bumper in his mouth, so read his body language now. A drop of the head may replace the closed mouth swallow. Pup will show you when he accepts this, so listen to what he is saying.

Our next problem occurs when Pup does sit as we commanded him, but he spits out the bumper of his mouth. Pup is either anticipating that we are going to send off for another bumper or he is challenging you by saying, "I'll sit for you, but I'm not going to sit and hold the bumper too." I have seen both responses many times and you do not need to worry about what Pup is telling you. The correction for either action is the same.

Any time this happens, quickly correct Pup with *NO-fetch!* Pup will pick up the bumper but he may attempt to hurry back after he does. Repeat the *NO-fetch* routine until he performs like we know he can. Be patient during this time—we are juggling conditioned and instinctive responses that can lead to a great deal of confusion in Pup's mind.

The final problem occurs when Pup gives us a cast refusal when we attempt to handle him with a *back* or *over* casts. This may manifest itself by Pup going in the wrong direction or by failing to cast at all. Use the corrections we have previously discussed to get out of trouble. Attrition, indirect e-collar pressure and even a tossed bumper may be used to get Pup going in the proper direction. My personal favorite is by taking a few steps in Pup's direction. This small reduction in distance intimidates dogs in a way that quickly regains control by you with no physical pressure.

Handling on the return is a skill that we will use in the field when communicating to Pup that he must engage the hazards when he returns as well as when he goes. Taking on heavy cover, not cheating around the water's edge, and running through "hot spots" where correction occurred can be easily attained if Pup is comfortable while being handled as he returns with a bumper or bird. However, the reason I handle dogs on the return is to prepare them for another drill, called swim-by. However, before we get wet there is one more drill that he needs to learn in the Double-T pattern.

FINISHED DOG

CHAPTER TWENTY-NINE

Do you want to use literal or momentum casting?

I attend many events each year handling my own dogs as well as those for my clients. My barometer when judging a handler and training program comes when they attempt to recover the blind retrieves. Some are precise with incredibly accurate casts while others are casual and sloppy. The precise teams invariably use a system termed literal casting. That is, the dog takes the literal angle his handler presents with his arm. It may be a forty-five degree angle arm position that sends the dog off on a perfect forty-five degree angle back. The angles are infinite, from a subtle five-degree back cast to an overt ninety degree over cast. All of these angles are learned in the Double-T pattern field. Literal casting will be our last stop at this venue.

Before we get into literal casting, let's look at another system called momentum casting. Go to any retriever event and you are likely to see a lot of momentum casting, especially from the amateur handlers. They may stick their arm out in an *over* position but give a verbal *back* cast in an effort to get Pup to take a forty-five degree angle cast. Visual casting (arm out in the over position) pushes their dog over. Verbal casting (*back*) pushes Pup back. The combination can result in the forty-five degree cast that the handler wants. It can also cause a lot of confusion in Pup's mind. He is thinking *back* and *over* at the same time. Why go there?

Which way should you go, literal or momentum? To answer that question, look in the mirror. We have not spoken about the handler's role in casting a dog until now. So, let's take a hard look at what Pup sees when he looks back to us for direction. Stand in front of a mirror and practice casting. How precise are you with your presentation? I am sure you will be sloppy at first, and then improve as you start to see how some of Pup's wrong casts may have been your fault. Now, stick your arm out in an *over* position and verbally cast *back*. Put yourself in Pup's place, and try to figure out what is correct. I hope you can visualize the confusion that momentum casting presents. It tells Pup to go one way, but shows him another.

The biggest complaint I have with momentum casting is that the handler who uses it is continually misleading Pup in one form or the other. If you lie to me, I will not trust you. Why should our dogs be any different? Do not lie to Pup. Literal casting says that if you will follow my lead (cast), it will take you directly to the bird. And, if you take it precisely enough, I will not stop you again before you find your reward. Let's face it— Pup does not like being corrected, with a whistle-stop and redirection. If you will be honest and use literal casting, Pup will trust you and be much more willing to follow your lead.

Up until now, we have been casting Pup either *over* or *back* in the pattern field. A literal casting dog is required to take varying degrees of angle *back* casts, and the easiest place to learn that skill is in the Double-T pattern. Pup knows the five spots that hold his rewards. Our job is to place Pup in position with whistle-stops that make learning the angle *back* casts to one of those five spots simple.

Begin by casting Pup from H to A without stopping. The next cast is from H to E, with a whistle-stop. Cast him over toward C, and whistle-stop again, halfway between E and C. Make sure you have Pup's total attention, and give him the correct angle *back* cast that will send him to A. Watch for a refusal as Pup will most likely want to go C. Use attrition, or toss a bumper to A, until he gets the message. A big concern is that Pup must never be rewarded if he refuses to take your cast. For that reason, there are no bumpers at C or B. The only place Pup can gain a reward is by taking our angle *back* casts to A. Repeat the process between E and B, using the correct arm angles when casting Pup to A.

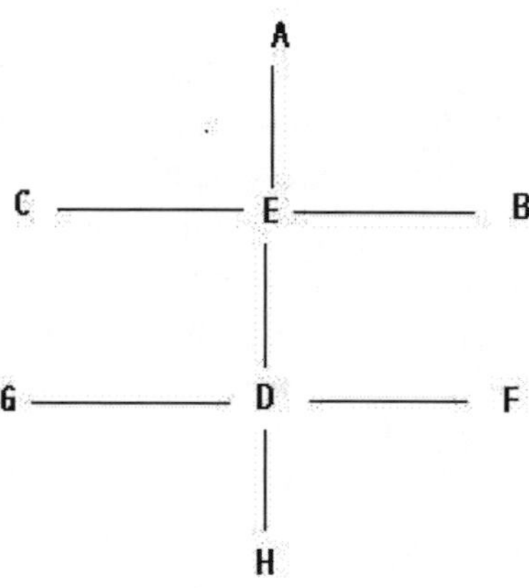

Vary the distance from E to B or E to C that you stop him, and you can condition virtually any angle with a cast to A. Soon, Pup will become quite confident, and you can expand his work into the rest of pattern. Whistle-stops between D and G or D and F will add distance when casting Pup at new angles to A. Later you can cast Pup from G or F to A with even greater angles. I draw the line on angle back casting when I can stop Pup at D and cast to either C or B without confusion. This dog is working hard for me.

FINISHED DOG

We have discussed angle backs to this point. What about the dog that runs past his bird and needs to be cast back in at an angle? Angle-ins are easily learned through the same method. Place bumpers at G and F. Whistle-stop Pup between D and E, and cast him with the proper arm angle to either G or F. Be patient until Pup is comfortable with this new idea.

The sky is the limit when learning angle back and angle in casts. You can create an infinite number of angles that will be quickly learned because of the pattern and Pup's confidence in you. I do not spend a lot of time on angle backs. After Pup shows me that he understands the concepts, I will reinforce the routine when we start running blinds in the open fields.

We are now finished with our Double-T pattern. It may be necessary to revisit the pattern when Pup shows us specific handling woes. You can always come back here if he is struggling with any of his casts and condition his responses to a higher degree. All handling problems can be cured in the Double-T pattern. Pup is comfortable here, and you are certain that he knows the routine. He will quickly accept the lessons and can learn what you need in short order. It is time to get wet, so let's go for a splash.

FINISHED DOG

CHAPTER THIRTY

Why does your dog handle well on land but struggle in water?

If you were to take a poll among people that participate in retriever events, a consensus opinion would rapidly form as to the most difficult portion of the events. Water blinds cause more stress among handlers than all the other tricks combined that judges throw at our dogs. Field trial water blinds used to be the great separator, because there were few drills to properly educate Pup on his water manners. With the advent of a drill termed “swim-by” water woes have become a thing of the past.

Swim-by takes what Pup learned in Double-T and applies the same skills to the water. It is the closest thing to magic I have seen for solidifying a dog’s trust and confidence in its handler. Before we can begin swim-by, there are several prerequisites. Pup must be well conditioned on his Double-T drill and handling just as well on his return as he does on the way out. Angle back casts should be confidently taken at any angle given by the handler. Pup must also be very comfortable working in the water. We take that for granted many times, but, before you begin swim-by, give Pup plenty of fun bumpers in the pond.

While we are on the topic of comfort, let’s talk about water temperature. During the swim-by drill, our student may be in the water for fifteen or twenty-minutes straight. If the water temperature in your pond is 35 degrees F, he will hate you, water and the drill when finished. It does not matter that your dog may love cold water and go jump into the pond for entertainment. Continually sending a dog into to cold water will cause problems, so don't do it. I can't give you a temperature that is safe, but somewhere in the fifties seems to cause little trouble in our pond. Do the hokey-pokey in your pond and judge for yourself.

Now, let's talk about the pond itself. You can run a swim-by drill anywhere there is water, but your efficiency will be greatly diminished if the dimensions and shape are not proper. My swim-by pond is a perfect rectangle shape, forty feet across and one hundred twenty feet wide. It is thirty inches deep throughout the entire pond. While no humans can walk on water, there are a few dogs at my kennel that believe I can.

It is doubtful that you will find such a pond around the corner from your house. I could not find anything close to what I needed for my daily work, so I dug one. That can be very expensive. However, I knew a guy that had an earth moving business and one day, he happened to need some dirt. I told him he could have my dirt if he would dig it out on my terms. In two days, I was in swim-by heaven. But, what if your bride tells you that you can have a swim-by pond or her, your choice? Take a close look at your marital situation and then call a local professional trainer. Ask if you can rent his pond until you finish this drill. He probably will not care and can offer help, for a fee, when needed.

Okay, you have all the bases covered and are ready to start swim-by with Pup. Where do we begin? In Double-T, there were five places where Pup could always find a reward. We want to reduce that by one in swim-by. There will be four places where Pup can enter and exit the water, and only four. We need to establish those to Pup and be sure that he understands them. The drill will look a great deal like Single-T on water.

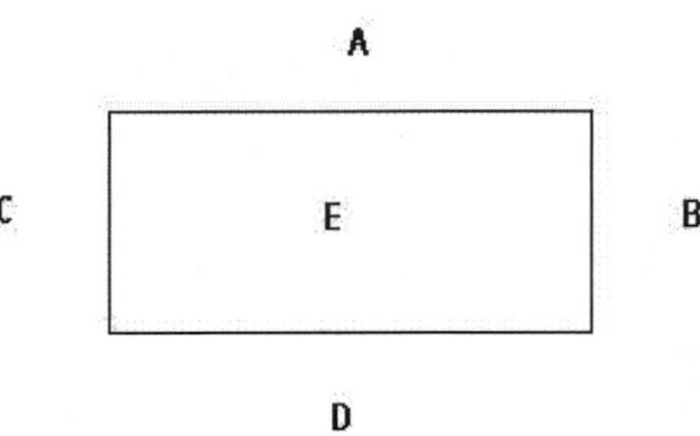

I begin swim-by by tossing fun bumpers from D into the pond and gradually extend the distance until Pup is moving freely from D to A. His return must be direct, that is, he cannot run around the pond. If Pup attempts this, stop him with your whistle and call him to you. Use attrition and *over* casting if necessary to show Pup his boundaries. Once he is comfortable going and coming from D to A, tackle the C to B line through the pond. This can be a little more challenging. Pup is required to swim a longer distance with the bank so close he can almost touch it. In my pond, Pup has to carry a forty-yard line in the water, while he is less than ten feet from the bank. Be prepared in case Pup tries to exit the water early. If he does exit at the wrong place, stop him with your whistle and cast him back into the middle of the pond. Then, call him to you with your whistle.

But, what if Pup will not cast into the water after minutes of attrition? Run around the pond until your position is directly on the opposite side of the pond from Pup. Then, call him back into the water. This is a short distance, and, if D to A went well, he should accept your command easily. When Pup is at the center of the pond, hustle back around to your original position and call him to you. This takes patience on your part. Keep your composure, and work with him until he is happily moving from D to A, C to B, and B to C. Begin with fun bumpers, and progress to where you require Pup to remain seated until sent by you.

This establishes the entrances and exits to Pup and will make the rest of the swim-by drill simple. When I began training swim-by, I did not spend much time working with the dogs on the four safe spots. My finished products were never as nice as the ones that we produce today. If Pup thinks that he can only leave the pond in one of four places, your use of attrition will quickly have Pup thinking you are a genius.

When the safe spots are well accepted by Pup, it is time to start the drill. Place a pile of bumpers at A, and send Pup from D to A until he is moving well. Now, send him from D to E, with a whistle-stop. Make sure he turns and looks at you while treading water. If Pup fails to tread by trying to swim back to you or turning on his own and heading for A, use your whistle and attrition casting (*tweet-tweet* or *back*) until he will tread water and await your cast. If you resolve this issue with Pup now, it is over. However, if you allow him to slip a few whistles here and there, you are rapidly training terminal habits into Pup.

After Pup will tread and await your cast, send him *back* to A. Congratulate him with a stroke on the shoulder and a hearty "Good dog!" when he does his job correctly. The wagging of his tail will tell you where the two of you stand. Now, send him from D to A without stopping. As with our land work, do not stop Pup with your whistle on successive sends to prevent popping. Now the fun begins.

Cast Pup from D to E, with a whistle-stop. Toss a bumper to B, and cast Pup *over* to the bumper. As he is swimming for B, run around the pond to C. When Pup picks up the bumper at B, call him back through the pond to you at C. After he delivers the bumper, congratulate Pup on a job well done ,and walk back to D for another D to A free run.

Send Pup from D to E again, with a whistle-stop. This time toss a bumper to C and cast Pup *over* to the bumper. Run around the pond to B, and call Pup to you from C to B. After delivery, walk back to D for another free run from D to A. Pup should now be comfortable going in either direction, so we will place bumper piles at A, B and C and cast him in the desired direction from this point forward.

Send Pup from D to E, with a whistle-stop. Cast him *over* to B. When he picks up the bumper at B, whistle-stop him and *over* cast Pup back into the pond to C. He should swim down the bank by you, all the way to C, and exit the pond at C. After he does this, call him to you with a hoop and holler. Then, repeat the routine from C to B. Work on these skills until Pup can cruise from one end of the pond to the other with no corrections.

Now, it is time for the finished swim-by drill. Place three bumpers at A. Send Pup from D to A without stopping him. Repeat D to A, and stop him with your whistle at the water's edge, on your side of the pond, when he returns. Cast him *back* into the water to A making, sure Pup takes the correct directional *back.* Whistle-stop him at A, and call Pup back to E, with a *tweet-tweet* and whistle-stop. As he treads, cast Pup *over* to B. At B, whistle-stop him and cast him *over*, into the pond, to C. When Pup gets to C, whistle-stop him and cast *over* back into the water to E. Whistle-stop Pup at E, and cast him *back* to A. Stop Pup again with your whistle at A, and *tweet-tweet* him back to you at D. Whew, that is a lot of casting. Now, send Pup from D to A, and welcome him back to you with lots of praise when he picks up the bumper.

When your dog can run the above sequence with no corrections, it's over. He trusts you completely and is doing things that are totally contrary to his natural instincts. This intense degree of conditioning rivals force fetching. Even Mr. Pavlov would have a hard time understanding how far we have taken the concept of conditioned responses with the swim-by drill.

Troubling problems on the swim-by drill can be endless if you did not prepare Pup well before coming here, or if you did not establish the entrance/exit spots (A, B, C, and D). The most common mistake by far occurs as Pup attempts to exit somewhere other than one of the four spots. This is relatively easy to correct, if Pup knows his handling skills, and, if he does not know them, you should not be here. If Pup is trying to exit on the far bank, stop him with your whistle, call Pup back into the middle of the pond, and repeat the cast he should have taken. Once again, attrition saves the day.

But, what if Pup tries to exit on the near side of the pond, hustling back to the safety of your side? Stop him at the water's edge with your whistle, and cast him back to the middle of the pond. Then, repeat the original cast. If Pup refuses to cast back into the pond, you have several choices, depending on whether Pup is e-collar conditioned.

For the non e-collar dog, run around the pond and call him back into the middle. Repeat the original command using attrition until Pup accepts. For the untrusting Pup, this can be an extremely handy time to have bumper in your back pocket. Toss a bumper to the opposite side of the pond, if necessary, to move Pup back out into the pond. Then, repeat your casting.

The e-collar has been used extensively in swim-by. For the properly conditioned dog, it is magic. Before using the e-collar, Pup should be forced into and out of the water, using the same system as we did during forcing to the pile. *Back-nick-back* should be conditioned at the water's edge on the near side of the pond as Pup is entering the pond, in the middle of the pond and at the water's edge on the far side of the pond as Pup is exiting the pond. This should be done without a bumper as Pup is on his way to retrieve and with a bumper in his mouth while you handle him on the return. *Over-nick-over* must be conditioned at spots E, B and C. Pup should be cast into and out of the water at B and C using *over-nick-over.* This entire process may take days or weeks depending on your dog's attitude. Pay close attention to Pup, and watch for the acceptance responses. Most importantly, toss a fun bumper when needed to keep him happy.

At some point during the drill, you will call Pup back in to you from A, and, when he reaches E, he will take a left or right turn and take off to C or B. This is called auto-swim-by. Pup is demonstrating how well conditioned we have made him through repetition. When you see this response, relax. The work is over, and he should cast easily to any of the four safe spots.

As you proceed through swim-by, find Pup's weaknesses. When he shows you a problem with a certain cast, spend a little extra time working on that cast in the next session. Just like we did in Double-T, if Pup leans to one direction, cast him to the other. We always lead and never follow— that is thc rolc of an alpha.

When you and Pup are confident with each other on the swim-by drill, take the show on the road to another body of water. Test the skills of swim-by at any new body of water until Pup shows you that he is bulletproof. Have Pup swim by you as he returns with a retrieve, instead of allowing a direct return. Handle him into and out of the water on both sides of the pond, while he has a bumper in his mouth. The dog that does this believes in you, and you should believe in him. Now Pup will cast as well on water as on land and, the rest of our handling drills will be all down hill.

CHAPTER THIRTY-ONE

How does Pup learn to take a good initial line?

To win a field trial or receive a high score in the noncompetitive tests, Pup must be comfortable running straight lines, not only on marks, but on blinds as well. Most every handler has a goal of "lining the blind" when they approach their blind retrieves, and this is what usually separates the dogs in their placements by the judges. In my judging experiences, I try to set up a blind that cannot be lined without whistle-stop and casting. Invariably, there will be a dog that takes that perfect line and carries it all the way to the blind without requiring any correction from the handler. It is quite impressive to see this trust in a dog to take on any hazard. Pup believes that his handler always tells him the truth. If Pup will go in the direction his handler sends him and remain on course, then there will be a reward for Pup. How do we attain that blind faith from our dogs?

Before we start to train our dogs to run straight, let's first look at what would make it easier for Pup to perform this skill. A lot of emphasis is placed on Pup's initial line as he leaves from our heel position. For this reason, he must be pointed in the proper direction not only with his head but also with his entire body. Lining a dog up before sending him to retrieve is accomplished by adjusting Pup's heel position until he is pointed in the correct direction. In our lining drills, we will fight a mighty battle with Pup until we get that desired heel position. And, only then, will we send Pup.

What are we trying to accomplish when we line Pup up in a direction? I have thought about this many times, and it took a lot of mind searching before I finally got down at Pup's level and took his position on this matter. Sitting on my rear end one day, after putting out a pile of blinds for a troubled student, I saw what I needed to understand. As we line Pup to release him on a blind or mark, he has many different points on the horizon that can attract his attention. Our job is to focus his attention on the spot where the blind retrieve is located. Correct heel position, good focus and running straight are the three requirements, so let's look at the drills that work on these skills.

Wagon wheel is a yard drill that will allow you to work on Pup's initial line in a small area. You and Pup will stand at the hub of the wheel, with a circle of bumpers around you. Initially, place bumpers at ninety-degree angles from each other located at positions A, B, C and D on the diagram. The distances from you to the bumpers can be ten yards or fifty yards, depending on what your training area offers. Whatever the distance, make sure the bumpers are clearly visible to Pup. I tend to start off in the ten-yard range and gradually build more distance as Pup's skills grow.

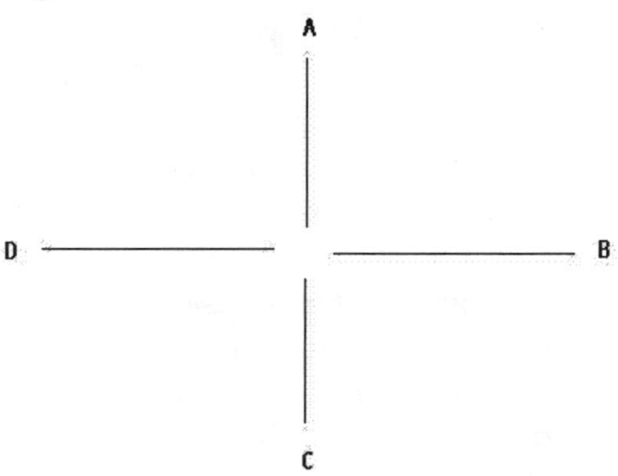

To begin the drill, use your heel position to line Pup up toward A. When he focuses on the bumper at A, place your hand in front of Pup's head and release him with a *back* command. When Pup returns from A, toss the bumper back to A. Now, line him up toward B and repeat the process in that direction. Then, move on to C and D. This is the beginning of wagon wheel, with four spokes in place. Pup should do these four spokes easily, since there are few hazards to divert his attention.

Before we add the other spokes in the wheel, let's talk about our timing when releasing Pup to go for the retrieve. Some people are of the opinion that we send Pup with a *back* as soon as our hand goes in front of his head. Others feel like they should hold their hand in front of Pup's face for an extended time before releasing him. I have successfully done it both ways with many different dogs. Initially, I will release Pup with my hand and verbal *back* as soon as he gives me the focus I am looking for. Later, as his skills grow, I like to hold Pup at heel for a few seconds, with my hand in front of his face pointing the way. With repetition, this will encourage Pup to focus in the proper direction. Be careful about starting this skill too soon. Holding an inexperienced dog too long can lead to a head swinging display by Pup that trainers call "buggy." Pup is nervous about going and refuses to focus in any direction. In his mind, if he does not focus, then he will not have to go. This is Pup's way of trying to get out of his job. He feels safer beside you than going to retrieve. Quick releases will get Pup moving again and should relieve his mental pressure, as he is successful on the retrieves.

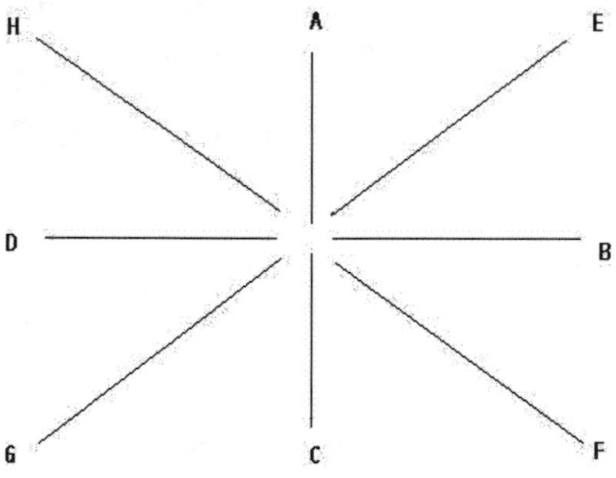

Now, we want to add more spokes to our wagon wheel at spots E and F. This presents a picture to Pup that is not so clear. When we are lining him up for F, he can also see C and B very clearly. Pup may decide to go for the wrong bumper as the picture clouds, and that's okay if he chooses the wrong bumper. He must learn to be comfortable while being corrected. Stop him with your whistle or verbal *no,* and call him back to your side.

Repeat the sends until he gets it right by going in the desired direction. Pup learned attrition during our casting drills and we will now use it on our lining drills also.

If you have used attrition multiple times and Pup still refuses to take the proper line, move forward and shorten the distance to the bumper. This will make the correct bumper the closest and give Pup a clearer view of the correct line. But, what if Pup still refuses to take the proper line? He must be corrected. For the non e-collar dog, stop him with the whistle. Give Pup a heavy *no* and call him back to you. Repeat the routine until he accepts your lead and takes the line you are giving him. For the e-collar trainer, stop him with your whistle. Give Pup a *nick* with the e-collar and call him back to you. As before, repeat the cast until he accepts.

Pay very close attention to Pup, and you will see when he accepts with his swallows. A lot of attitude can be lost if this drill becomes too heavy in Pup's mind. Keep an eye on his enthusiasm and focus. If either fades, slow down and move closer to the bumper in an effort to help Pup.

When Pup can easily line to spots A, B, C, D, E and F, then add G and H. This will give you eight spokes on the wheel and offer Pup distractions on both sides when you send him to retrieve. I like to move around the wheel, taking them in order (A, H, D, E, etc.) on my first pass. On the second pass around the wheel, I will skip every other bumper, picking up A, D, B and C while skipping H, E, G and G. On the third pass, I will pick up E, F, G and H while skipping B, C, A and D. Make sure to replace the retrieved bumpers back in their original positions, so they can offer Pup the distractions needed. It is likely that Pup will want to chase the bumper you tossed back out. As he focuses on that bumper, command him *No* and move on to the next bumper that you want him to retrieve. This is a version of the *No-No* drill where Pup learns to accept *No* and follow your lead.

After he can handle the *No* drill, we will leave off the *No* and simply change his line with our heel position. Now, Pup is accepting our lead without correction. When Pup returns with a bumper, you should already be lined up in the direction for his next retrieve. Send him in the desired direction after he lines up to deliver. Do not accept delivery until Pup is lined up in the proper direction and focused on the correct bumper. Should Pup decide to look in another direction, move forward until he gets the picture. This drill usually progresses very quickly, and it is not uncommon for a dog to be happily completing it in just a few days. However, don't be in a hurry. What is the big deal if it takes your Pup two weeks to get it right? As with all of our training, go at Pup's pace.

Some trainers will take wagon wheel to another level by placing another ring of bumpers outside our first circle. The line to each of the new bumpers is between our initial spokes. Typically, the outside ring consists of orange bumpers. This requires Pup to run past close and very visible white bumpers to the less visible orange bumpers. I do not run this drill unless Pup is struggling with running past hazards in the field. If he continually runs back to old falls or easily falls for distractions, then I come back to the wagon wheel and add an outside ring.

Be careful, as this can quickly become a heavy *No-No* drill with a big loss in momentum.

When Pup can comfortably go around the wagon wheel in the above drills, it is time to add some distance to Pup's line with a long line drill. This drill will begin with three lines and then progress to five lines of distances from 200 to 300 yards. Let your training grounds determine the length and hazards you present Pup. I like to have Pup run through ditches, ponds, roads and heavy cover. Or, he may be required to run past hay bales, bird stations, bird crates, telephone poles, people or another dog. Both distance and hazards are being addressed in this drill, and Pup must learn to ignore both by running in a straight line to his rewards.

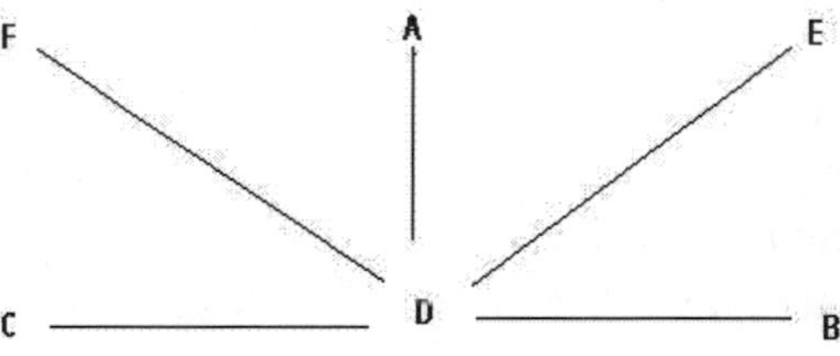

Start by placing a pile of bumpers at A, B and C. You and Pup assume a position at D. Run the legs to A, B and C as blinds initially. Continue to repeat these lines until Pup can line them (go directly to them without being stopped). This may take a week or two, so be patient. Do not allow Pup to run around any of the hazards. If he chooses to avoid them, handle him through the hazards while keeping him on the proper line. Repeat the same blind until Pup carries his line past and through all the hazards.

If Pup is struggling with this drill, move closer to A, B and C until he is comfortable. Then, back up as Pup's momentum and attitude dictate. With some dogs I have been required to start ten yards from A, B, C and then back up the remaining two hundred or so yards over the period of a week. Your point of emphasis is that Pup must be exact in his lines to the blinds. If he varies in the least, use his handling skills to correct his line and keep him going straight. Then, repeat the same blind until Pup will carry his line all the way to that blind. Remember, Pup does not like to be stopped and cast. That equates to a correction in his mind, and he would rather avoid correction if there is another option. Show Pup that his option is to accept your line and go straight. I have repeated the same blind six or seven times before some Pups would accept. Don't worry if your dog does the same.

When Pup can run A, B and C without a hitch, add E and F to the mix. I like to have their distances fifty or so yards longer than A, B and C. Now, Pup is being asked to carry some very long distances with many hazards. Use the handling skills of whistle-stop, attrition, verbal correction, e-collar correction and repetition until Pup easily takes these five lines. This is a good time to really reinforce your heel position and holding your hand in front of Pup's face until he focuses on the proper line.

We spoke of head swinging earlier in this chapter, and I cannot think of a dog that did not swing his head at some time during this drill. Usually a *No-here* and hand alignment will focus Pup in the proper direction. But, the occasional dog may refuse to give you the focus that is necessary. For these problem students, I like to place a white bucket at the bumper pile. The bucket gives Pup something to focus on and will make his job much easier. Some trainers will scoff at the use a bucket saying that the bucket will cause Pup to fall into traps later on, because he will want to run to anything white in the field. If we did not train any further on this, I would agree. We will do a diversion drill later on that will take this temptation away from Pup. Make it easy for Pup to learn, and then take away his training wheels. After he knows how to do the skill, he can and will run without the aid of a bucket. Contrary to the non-bucket trainers, I know of a few very good field trial trainers that run every blind to a bucket throughout the dog's entire training career. The only time their dogs run a blind without the bucket is at an event. They usually perform very well and boy, do these dogs run with style.

When your dog has completed the lining work, your job as a handler will be much easier. Pup will now be comfortable taking your line in any direction, through almost any hazard. Before you know it, Pup will be lining the majority of your training blinds and you will look like a hero to your training partners. More importantly, Pup will trust you with blind faith.

FINISHED DOG

CHAPTER THIRTY-TWO

Why do we cast Pup around the wagon wheel?

Whether you intend to train your dog for hunting or event work, Pup will be required to handle in the face of many complex distractions. Judges at the field events love to place as many hazards as possible in Pup's way, in an effort to evaluate his ability to work with the handler. The dog that ignores the hazards and readily follows his handler will take home a lot of ribbons in his career. Likewise, the hunting dog continually experiences distractions. A friend and I were discussing this recently, and we both agreed that a good hunt probably provides more confusion from the dog's perspective than any field trial ever could.

Because of this, we want to go back to the wagon wheel one more time, in an effort to refine our casting skills. There will be many times when Pup's instincts tell him to go in one direction, but our needs are in another. Good casting skills that have been well conditioned are necessary at these times. Casting Pup around the wagon wheel is one of the best drills I know to condition responses in the face of distraction. It requires very little space, and the sessions are typically short, so Pup does not become physically or mentally exhausted.

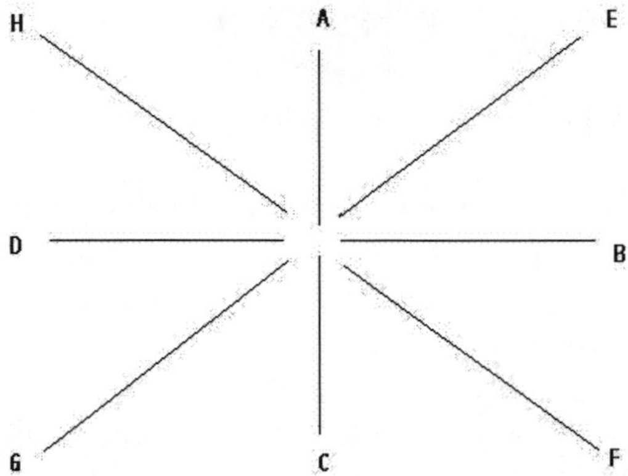

We will begin in the same manner as our previous wagon wheel drill, with bumpers at A, B, C, and D. Pup will be in the middle at the hub, but now we will be outside of the wheel. Cast Pup back to A, using first your left hand then your right, making sure he takes the correct directional backs. Use a *tweet-tweet* to bring Pup in and pick up the bumper at B. Cast him left or right for bumpers at C and D. In the small space, this can be confusing for Pup, but it is a great way to polish your casting skills when Pup follows your lead.

When Pup can handle A, B, C and D, it is time to add the other spokes at E, F, G and H. Now, you can work on angle backs to G and H or angle-ins at F and E. This is a finesse drill and requires patience on your part as a handler. Pup is going to make mistakes. Understand this when you begin, and do not expect perfect work for a while. When Pup does make a mistake, use attrition as your primary correction tool until Pup accepts your cast.

For the e-collar trainer, be a little more patient than normal. There is a tremendous amount of confusion in this drill. Remember that we do not want to add pressure to Pup when he is feeling pressure. So, give Pup a few more attempts with attrition before using e-collar correction. Some dogs will no-go in this drill, due to the volume of confusion. Keep an eye on this, and a bumper in your back pocket just in case Pup needs a little help.

Five or ten minutes of this drill each day will quickly condition a dog to follow your lead, even when his instincts tell him to go his own way. Now, we have a dog that lines and casts in the face of great distractions. We have one more drill, and then we are off to the field to show the world Pup's new skills.

CHAPTER THIRTY-THREE

Should you run field blinds before mastering the diversion drill?

To this point, Pup has learned a lot about handling and following your casts, even when his gut tells him to go on another course. All of his training has revolved around handling past areas where he knows there may be another bumper or bird for him. But, in each of these cases, he did not see a bird fall, and he was in an area where a great deal of conditioning occurred. When Pup runs his first field blind, it is doubtful that his view of where we want him to go will be clear. Pup may want to run to an area where he picked up a marked retrieve. We need a communication system where he will be comfortable when we redirect his focus, and this is done with a diversion drill.

Begin the drill by placing a pile of bumpers at A. I like to have my distance from B to A set at around 100 yards, but do what your training grounds allow. Run Pup on a blind retrieve from B to A until he lines the blind with confidence. This may take two or three casts or two or three days. Do not go forward until Pup is flying from B to A with excellent momentum.

Now we need some assistance from a helper. Place him about ten yards off to the side of Pup's line to the blind in a holding blind at C, about two-thirds of the way out to A. Your helper needs to take a few things to the blind with him— a duck call, a loaded gun, two dead birds and a live bird. With your helper and his equipment in the holding blind, send Pup from B to A again. If he should look to your helper, use your lining skills to redirect Pup's attention to A and send him. You may have to handle him with whistle-stops and casts if he veers off course. Send Pup from B to A until he pays no attention to your helper in the blind.

Next, have your helper step out of the blind in view of Pup. This should get Pup's attention and he is likely to expect your helper to throw a bird for him. Command Pup *No* and realign him toward A. Send him to A, and handle with whistle and casts if he does not take a direct line to A. Repeat the sends until Pup lines to A without acknowledging your helper.

With this done, have your helper appear and blow a duck call. *No* Pup off your helper and send him from B to A. As before, handle and repeat until Pup is going from B to A without hesitation. By now, he should be getting the idea.

Now have your helper appear, blow his duck call and fire the gun. This should have Pup's full attention. Again, command *No,* realign Pup in the direction of the bumper pile, and send him from B to A. Pup should handle this comfortably now and go directly to A without any problem.

When he is comfortable with the last scenario, have your helper appear, blow his duck call, throw a dead duck, and fire the gun. Pup should be locked on the thrown bird. Send him for the bird by calling his name. When he returns with the bird, line him up facing A before taking delivery of the bird. After Pup delivers, send him from B to A.

On our next scenario, we will challenge Pup a little more. Have your helper appear, blow his duck call, throw a dead bird and fire the gun. While Pup is focused on the thrown bird, command him *No* and realign him facing A. Instead of releasing Pup for the bird, send him for a bumper at A. Pup may decide to veer toward the bird. If he does, handle him away from it to the bumper pile at point A. If Pup does waver, repeat this until he lines from B to A without looking at the thrown bird. When he returns from A with the bumper, line him up facing the thrown bird, and send him for it by calling his name.

Pup has the idea when he can complete the last step successfully. One more piece in the diversion drill puzzle is all that is left. Have your helper appear, blow his duck call, throw a live bird and shoot it. Pup's attention will be riveted to the bird. Command *No* and realign him facing A. Send him from B to A to the bumper pile. Hopefully by now, Pup understands, and, even with a shot flyer in his face, he will follow our lead. If he should falter, handle him to A and repeat the drill until he takes your line from B to A with total trust in you. When he returns from A with the bumper, line him for the flyer and send him for it with his name.

After he completes this drill, tell him what a good dog he is by throwing a few fun bumpers and loving him on the shoulders. Pup now has the skills to run any poison bird blind a judge might present or any hunting situation may require. We are ready to head to the fields or ponds and run some blinds in the wide-open spaces. It may be necessary for us to revisit some of our handling drills if Pup should show us repeated weaknesses, but it will be easy for him to quickly recover from his faults. These drills may have been time-consuming and, at times, boring, but the skills Pup now possesses will be with him for his lifetime. Pup should trust you and understand that you will never place him in jeopardy. If he follows your lead, there will always be a reward in the form of a bumper or bird waiting for him.

FINISHED DOG

CHAPTER THIRTY-FOUR

Why won't pattern blinds cause Pup problems?

Before we answer this question, let's explain what pattern blinds are. They are spots in the open field where Pup is likely to find a blind retrieve located. We may run the same pattern blind four or five days in a row, in an effort to train Pup on a concept that, otherwise, would be difficult to master. "Repeat blinds" is probably a better term but most trainers call them pattern blinds.

There are some trainers who believe we should never repeat a mark or a blind retrieve. They believe that repeating these scenarios will encourage Pup to return to an old area. This is a serious fault in most people's book, and the reason many trainers refuse to run this drill. However, after mastering the diversion drill, Pup should not have a problem with accepting your direction into any area. So, where's the problem?

On the flip side, what is the benefit of repeating pattern blinds? Any time we transfer skills from one area to another, most dogs will show a lack of confidence or momentum. This is especially true when we move into the open field and ask Pup to run a blind retrieve. Repeating a blind will most likely cause Pup to return to the spot with both momentum and enthusiasm. After Pup learns the spot, we can change our point of origin and run to the same pattern blind location from another starting point. What a great way to introduce a complex blind to a young dog. Running a blind under the arc of a marked retrieve, through the fall of an earlier mark or close to the bird station can present a lot of problems to any dog. But, if Pup is comfortable running a pattern blind to a certain location, asking him to perform the above skills will be much easier. He knows where to go to be successful— it is our job to be patient and handle him until he gets there. With enough repetition, Pup will pay little attention to the hazard and proceed easily through the hazard to the blind.

So, if you choose to take the benefits of pattern blinds, where do we begin? I like to set up my pattern blinds in area where I can expand both distance and angle. Some of these blinds will be in the middle of a field, while others may be on the edge of the woods. Choose the spots that will fit your training area and place a pile of bumpers along with a visual marker for yourself and Pup. I use a fluorescent orange stake and place a white milk container on top of the stake initially. This will give Pup something to focus on as he learns the drill and can bail him out, should he become lost in the middle of a blind.

With everything in place, there are several ways to begin running the drill. First, you can back off as far as possible and have a helper throw a mark to the pile. When Pup returns successfully with the mark, send Pup back to the spot again on a blind retrieve. He will likely carry to the bumper pile with ease, but be prepared to cast Pup using the skills learned in previous chapters, should he falter. I used to use this method a great deal but recently have switched to a simpler approach.

Now, I prefer to start Pup running his first pattern blinds from a very short distance, say twenty yards. As Pup becomes confident and successful by lining to the bumper pile with ease, then I back up until the desired distance is accomplished. Some dogs can learn to carry two hundred yards in one day while others require several days before they can line the blind at long distances. Another benefit to this method is that you can introduce hazards (cover, terrain changes, ditches, ponds, etc.) one at a time along the way. If Pup struggles, you can go back to where he was last successful and repeat the blind from a point where he is confident before backing up again.

The last method and least desirable, in my opinion, is to start Pup at your end point and simply run the blind cold. This can lead to poor momentum and a great deal of confusion from our student. It usually requires a great deal of casting and whistle-stops before Pup finds the bumper pile. When he returns, repeat the blind until he can line it without hesitation. This works, but is a little more difficult for Pup, so pay close attention to his attitude.

In any case, whichever method you choose, demand that Pup remain on the correct line while he is on the way to the bumper pile. Should he veer off course, stop him with your whistle and use the correct cast to put him back on line. This is where literal casting is of great benefit. It is also a wonderful way to reinforce the literal casts that we introduced to Pup back in Double-T. If Pup takes the literal cast that we give him, he will not be stopped again before he finds his prize. Think about this from Pup's view. He does not like to be stopped with the whistle. That means he has made a mistake and we are correcting him. With enough repetition, he will understand and, more importantly, accept the exact cast that we choose with our arm angle. What if out student does not take the correct cast? Go back to attrition casting and use whatever corrective means (verbal or e-collar) Pup is conditioned to accept. I normally give a dog many chances when introducing pattern blinds before any physical corrections occur. This is new turf for him, and aggressive corrections can lead to a huge loss of momentum.

When Pup does successfully pick up the bumper at the pile, the control does not stop there. Insist that Pup return directly on line to you without running around or flaring from any hazards. Now, I hope you can see the importance of handling on the return in our Double-T drill. If you allow Pup to flare on his return, it is likely that he will try that same flare on his back out to the bumper pile when you repeat his next blind. Cut him off at the pass by not allowing him to begin flaring. Should he try this, stop him with your whistle, and handle him back to the spot where he left the proper line. Then, call him to you, making sure he remains on line.

After you and Pup master the first pattern blind, it is time to add as many as your training area allows. I have from three to seven in most of my training fields or ponds. Take your time introducing them, and continue the repetition until he can line the pattern blind of your choice without hesitation.

With these pattern blinds in place, run your marking pattern in the same training areas. Now you are asking Pup to pick up his marks in a pattern that he understands, and then run a pattern blind that he also understands. Transition from the yard to the field can be very hard on Pup mentally, but this method should make the transition easier.

So far, we have talked about this on land. When your land work has been mastered, then repeat the same routine on water. I prefer to start on land and then go to water after Pup demonstrates that he has the skills. Land corrections are much easier for us than water corrections in Pup's early training, so let's keep it simple for both dog and trainer.

When setting up water pattern blinds, I try my best to incorporate as many concepts as possible. I begin by having Pup swim past a point on his early water blinds. When he demonstrates the ability to do this, I require Pup to carry his casts down a bank at a close distance to the bank. From here, we will send Pup across a point of land back into the water on his way to the bumper pile. Use whatever your training area offers to educate Pup on what he must do to satisfy you. Keep the angles open and simple at first by not asking Pup to get too close to the banks or points. As he shows you that he can handle this, change your point of origin and tighten the lines up until Pup can carry his line within a few feet of the banks or points without hesitation.

With all of this accomplished, Pup should be willing and able to follow your lead with almost any cast. If you took your time and went at a pace where Pup was glad to accept your presentations, his confidence and momentum should be excellent. Too much mental or physical pressure will show itself quickly in Pup's attitude. Let him tell you when to move forward, or even back, on those troublesome days. Handling Pup around a field or in a pond is easy now, so let's move on to some advanced degrees with our student.

CHAPTER THIRTY-FIVE

What makes Pup want to cheat?

One of the first books I read about training retrievers was Bill Tarrant's Hey Pup, Fetch it Up!. He has a story in the book about a day when he and a friend were hunting. They shot a bird that disappeared over the pond's dam. The dog was sent and took a perfect line through the pond, over the dam and out of sight. A few minutes later, the dog came back to them with the bird. Bill's friend was very complimentary about what a nice job the dog had done handling a difficult situation with relative ease. Bill, on the other hand, was disappointed, much to his friend's disbelief. It seems that Pup made a great retrieve, but, on his return, decided to take the easy way out around the pond instead of through it. Mr. Tarrant felt like the dog cheated him by not doing the job exactly right. Every time I watch a dog cheat and attempt to take the easy way, I think about Bill Tarrant and that story.

What made Mr. Tarrant's dog want to cheat around the pond instead of coming directly back to him on the same path he took going to the bird? I have many people come and train with us. At some point, they all ask the question of why a dog would continue to choose a path where he knows I will correct him, instead of going in a direct route? My reply is simple, "How did you get to my property today?" The response is that they drove on the road. I come back with, "So, you took the easy path instead of the direct route." Instinct in all animals tells them to follow the path of least resistance, and all dogs will do this when retrieving, until conditioned to run in a straight line.

A lot of you are ready to skip this chapter and move on since you do not care if Pup runs straight as long as he brings the bird back. I do not totally disagree with you. However, there will be times when you need Pup to go straight for his safety or just because that is what a finished dog should do. If Pup is allowed to run off line, let it be by our choice and not his.

How do we instill into Pup's mind that taking on the hazards and running straight is what pleases us? We have done that, to some degree, with our pattern blinds, but now we want to present big hazards and big temptations to run around those hazards at the same time. I go back to my swim-by pond to stop the cheating process. Standing at A, I will have a helper throw a mark to B and send Pup for the retrieve. This angle is not too severe, and he should take the correct path with little trouble. When he picks up the mark, make sure he returns in a direct line without cheating on his return. Use your handling skills to adjust his position. Repeat the mark if necessary until Pup gets the idea.

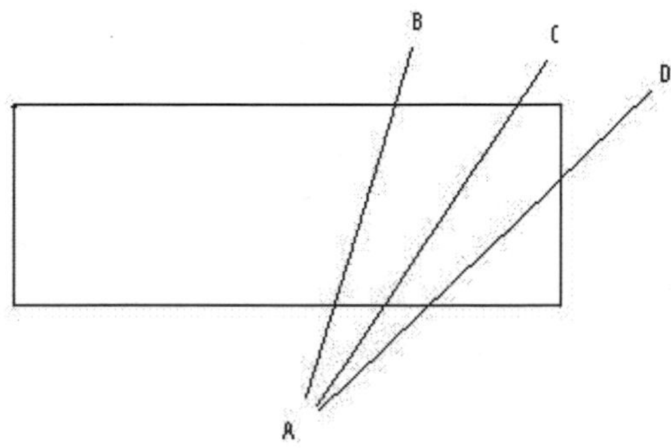

Next, we are going to run Pup from A to C until he can negotiate the angles offered. A little more patience from you is needed here. He is likely to try a trip around the pond, instead of going directly out and back. As before, handle him to the correct spot, when necessary. Repeat A to C until you get that perfect response.

Now, let's have your helper toss his mark to D. Send Pup from A to D, making sure he stays on the correct line. At this angle, he will challenge you by running around the pond. Stop him with your whistle, call him back and repeat the mark. What if Pup still refuses to go straight, even after many attempts? For the non e-collar dog, use heavy verbal correction, after whistle-stopping Pup at the pond's corner. Do not correct him as he leaves your side. He may think that going is what gets him into trouble and start no-going. Instead, let him get to the corner of the pond and then correct him. He will understand that his location is what caused the problem and not his going to retrieve. Call Pup back and handle him with whistle and voice on the proper line to the bird. The e-collar dog is corrected in the same manner with a *nick* at the pond's corner. Watch for the swallow response in both cases when Pup says, "I accept."

When Pup can handle the above drill, it is time to add some challenge by backing up both the starting point and the marks from the pond's edge. Distances can be short in the beginning but need to approach one hundred yards at the end. The same rules apply now as before, but the temptations are larger. There is a whole lot more land on which Pup can run around. Use all your skills to keep him on line and happy. Start with B, progress to C and then D as he accepts the routine. When you finish this, Pup should be able to take any angle entry or exit that the toughest judges could set up.

Until now we have taken on angles. It is time to take thin slices of the pond next. Change your starting point to A, and have your helper throw the mark to B. If all has gone well to this point, Pup should carry his line through the pond. As before, when he fails, correct his line with your handling skills and repeat the process until Pup performs correctly. When he can successfully complete this, move your helper back and have B some distance (20 to 100 yards) past the pond's edge. After Pup does this well, back up until A is 20 to 100 yards from the pond's edge.

Now, it is time to repeat this concept in other places. Go to as many different ponds as possible and ask Pup to take the challenging angles in and out of the pond. Don't be afraid to repeat the same mark as many times as needed to gain the control and directness you desire. Pup should be bulletproof by now and ready to take on any handling situation a judge or mallard can present.

FINISHED DOG

CHAPTER THIRTY-SIX

What does Pup learn in a multiple-blind drill?

There is one more drill that we need to discuss before we close the toolbox on handling. It is used to troubleshoot any handling problems or as a way to maintain Pup's casting skills away from the pattern field. Many dogs will become perfect students in Double-T, but challenge you in the field. The multiple-blind drill gives you a tool that will expand Pup's horizons. It is the culmination of all the handling skills. Some trainers call it a Chinese drill, because it can resemble a Chinese fire drill, with both Pup and handler becoming confused. The confusion is a good thing, because Pup will learn to recover from this state in a successful manner when he follows your lead.

We call this a multiple-blind drill because there will be from three to seven blinds in the field at different locations. I try to vary the angles and distances of each blind so that Pup is required to completely follow my lead, or he will be unsuccessful. This drill will also clean up some of the desire Pup has to run back to an old fall that was created by repeating our pattern blinds. We will not repeat any of these blinds. He gets one chance to do it right.

When setting up a multiple-blind drill, I let the land or water determine where the bumpers are placed. In small areas, I may only be able to locate three spots. In large open fields, you should be able to add five or seven blinds. This is a time when I try to stretch Pup out as far as possible, so the distances are set from one hundred to four hundred yards. Set the blinds up like bowling pins in staggered positions from each other, and add as many hazards to the mix as your training area allows. Because of the distance and volume, it can take a long time to complete this drill, and Pup will most likely be quite tired when finished. I have known a few handlers that had a problem blowing their whistle before all the blinds were retrieved because they ran out of air when running this drill. So, run it very slowly and deliberately.

FINISHED DOG

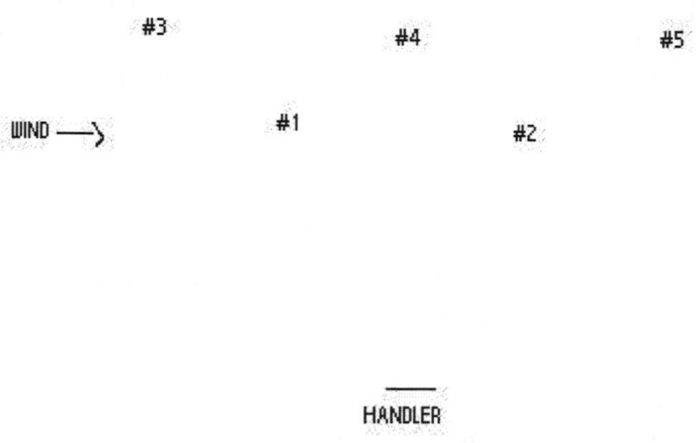

In our diagram, we will demonstrate a five-leg drill, with the wind blowing from left to right. We will start by picking up the nearest upwind blind, which in our diagram is #1. Line Pup up using his lining skills, and send him for #1. He should handle this one with ease, as there will be little confusion in his mind. When he returns, line him up for #2 before taking delivery. As he delivers, immediately send him for #2 without a great deal of fuss over his line. Now the fun begins, as he will probably lean back toward #1. Use your whistle-stop and casting skills to handle Pup all the way to #2.

From #2, we send Pup for the long upwind blind at #3. After #3, we take out #4. It will be the most difficult as our student must now negotiate a path between #1 and #2 while not heading back to #3 where he just found a reward. Finish the session by picking up the long downwind blind at #5. We start upwind and work down to allow Pup's nose to work. But, even with his nose smelling the old areas, he must still follow our lead to a spot away from where his instincts tell him to go.

Initially, the multiple-blind drill is not a lining drill. We want to focus on casting while having Pup concentrate on us. Send him for the next blind by simply lining him up at heel and releasing. When Pup's casting skills are honed, then we will come back to this drill and devote a session to his lining skills.

We are going to change the way we cast in our multiple-blind drill. We will slow down the process by counting to five after Pup stops on the whistle and before giving Pup his cast. This will require Pup to focus on us. If he should swing his head or look for his own path, count to ten. Do not cast him until you have Pup's total attention. This is also a time to be extremely literal in your casting. By slowing down, you can concentrate on your arm angle. The majority of the dogs I train become much more literal in their casting after we run this drill a few times, so be patient.

It is inevitable that Pup will give you some cast refusals in these sessions. The drill is designed to cause confusion that will make him want to follow his instincts instead of us. When the refusals occur, use the attrition system until you get the exact cast you are looking for. Pup must turn the proper direction and take the angle you gave him or you will call him back to where the refusal occurred. From there, you will repeat the cast until he accepts your lead by taking the cast. Now, I hope you can see how much time this drill may require. But, this is time well spent.

For argument's sake, let's say our student refuses to take the cast after many attempts. What do we do? With a non e-collar dog, I shorten the distance between Pup and me by walking out toward him. Most dogs are threatened by this action to a degree that straightens their act up. You are working at extreme distances, and Pup may think he does not have to listen when so much ground separates the two of you. Show Pup that you can come "visit" him if you need to, and I am sure he will pay a little more attention to your next cast. After you have walked out toward Pup a few times and gotten your point across, a few simple steps in his direction will accomplish the same thing. Watch his head drop, and look for the swallow responses. As those happen, you can stop walking because Pup is telling you that he understands.

For the e-collar dog, use the same system that has been in place from the beginning. After repeated cast refusals, stop Pup with your whistle as he takes the incorrect cast. As he is seated, *nick* him with the e-collar, and call Pup back to where the cast refusal occurred. Reseat him with your whistle, and repeat the proper cast. If you did your homework, Pup should take the cast with understanding and enthusiasm. Watch for his posture changes and swallows as Pup tells you he accepts.

I have not mentioned whistle-stop problems in a long time. I bring the topic up now because some dogs may skip a whistle or two in this drill. If this occurs more than once in a session, you probably should not be here. I would suggest that you go back to Double-T or pattern blinds to correct the whistle refusals. Stay away from the multiple-blind drill until Pup is bulletproof on these skills. This drill will quickly become mass confusion if you have to fight with Pup over whistle-stops and exact casting through old areas. So, don't be in a hurry to get here.

After Pup can comfortably run a multiple-blind drill on land, take the show to your ponds and repeat the process in water. Concentrate on having Pup carry his casts by points, down banks and across points. Arrange your setup so that he must also carry some of the casts out of the ponds for some distance. Running a seven-leg drill on water can take a very long time, so pay close attention to the temperature of the water. Also, you might want to pack a lunch for yourself.

We have focused primarily on casting to this point. You can also use this drill as a way to improve Pup's lining skills. Previously, we spent little or no time lining Pup up because our focus was on casting. If our student is having lining problems, use the multiple-blind drill as you did the wagon wheel drill, by having Pup focus on his line. This requires a lot of patience from you. If Pup does not take the correct line and hold it, stop him with your whistle and call him back to heel. Realign him and send Pup again. This can be very tiring for you and Pup, but there are great rewards in precise lines when Pup does accept. Watch for his cues.

Quite often, dogs become confused in their work. Very few drills will be as confusing to Pup as the multiple-blind drill. Take your time when running this drill, and when finished, Pup will be able to handle any cast or line, no matter how great the confusion.

CHAPTER THIRTY-SEVEN

Why does Pup go to school to learn multiple marks?

When things go well in the duck blind, pheasant field or goose pit, a group of birds will present themselves to the guns. At some point, Pup will see more than one bird fall, and he must learn to handle this scenario with comfort. When hunting, multiple marks do occur on a regular basis. In any retriever event but the most basic stake, Pup is required to mark and remember more than one bird, so what is the easiest way for him to learn this skill?

HANDLER

When training a dog on multiple marks, I send Pup to "school." By this, I mean that I will "school" Pup on his memory bird as a single retrieve before adding the second bird to form a double. In the diagram above, I will have Pup pick up a single at #2 on his initial retrieve. When he returns, my helper will throw mark #2 again, and another helper will throw mark #1. Pup will be focused on #1, so I send him for it by calling his name. When he returns with #1, I line him up for #2 before taking delivery. After delivery, I wait for him to focus on #2 and, only then, send him for #2. He has already been successful at #2 on the earlier single, so getting him to go back to that area should not be too difficult. This is the first step in "schooling" Pup on multiple marks.

In the beginning, the angle between #1 and #2 should be great and the distances short. I have been known to expose the memory bird by having it placed in an area with little or no cover. This allows Pup to find the bird quickly and with little effort, elevating his confidence. Another approach that works well is to place many bumpers in the area of the memory bird. Most people call this "seeding" the area of the fall. He should find one of the bumpers without having to hunt for an extended time. The key to multiple marks is having Pup successfully complete them while remaining confident. "Schooling" is my favorite way to stroke Pup's confidence and ensure that he will be successful.

With young or inexperienced dogs, confusion can occur when you ask Pup to go for his memory bird. I have seen them look off into space, as if they do not remember that there is another bird out in the field. Each time I see this happen, I ask the bird thrower to help Pup out of this mess. First, my helper steps out exposing his position and catching Pup's attention. Often, this is all that is required to get Pup focused back into the correct area. If Pup does not refocus after my helper shows himself, I ask the helper to blow his duck call in an effort to gain Pup's focus again. Even with this, some dogs will hesitate. For them, I have my helper call Pup out to the correct area by saying "Hup, Hup, Hup" and backing up until Pup comes into the area and finds the bird. Our student should go ballistic when he hears "Hup, Hup, Hup" and eagerly head in the correct direction. He learned this process in our early fieldwork and should remember a reward awaits him.

Now, we need to go back and repeat the entire process until Pup can happily run the double. Some dogs will pick this up very quickly and need no repeat drills. Others will struggle, and you may be required to repeat the same double four or five times before Pup figures out the puzzle. In my experience, I have seen little difference in the finished product. Most of the dogs that struggled with their initial multiples went on to become excellent markers after training. We are training Pup to become confident in himself. Some dogs are born with lots of confidence (alphas), and others learn to become confident by going to "school." Either way, he will be successful.

As Pup demonstrates that he can handle simple doubles, add some distance and tighten the angles. This will move the birds further away from you and Pup, but closer to each other. Now, Pup is required to concentrate a little more on where the birds are located. This will lead us into concept marks a little later. Any failures will be handled as before, with help from our bird thrower and repetition until Pup is successful.

Before we talk about concepts, Pup should learn to comfortably perform triples. We will take what Pup learned in doubles and add another bird to form the triple. From the diagram above, start by schooling Pup on bird #1 as a single. Next, run Pup on a double, with birds at #1 and #2. This is open, so Pup should be comfortable. If he is not, repeat the routine until he is happily performing the double. Now, repeat the double and add bird #3 to form a triple. In the beginning, I like to have the distance to #3 short. This will make Pup's job easy and open the triple up in Pup's view. With bird #3 retrieved, birds #1 and #2 are separated by a great distance. Pup was schooled on these marks earlier, so he should have little trouble completing the triple. If he does struggle, have your helper lend a hand and repeat the routine until Pup's tail is wagging his body.

From this point, you can continue to add as many marks to the multiple as your situation mandates. Some retriever events require quadruple marks, so, if you plan to play that game, prepare for it. I have heard trainers speak of their dogs comfortably remembering and retrieving as many as seven marks. If that is what meets your goals, go for it.

Any time you present Pup with more than one marked retrieve, there is some form of a concept that he must resolve. Each of these concepts presents Pup with a visual problem that he must master, and this is accomplished through repetition of the concept until Pup becomes comfortable. Let's look at the most common concepts, and try to understand what Pup sees in them.

The basic triple that we demonstrated before, is called an "inline triple," because each of the bird throwers and bird locations are in a straight line with each other. By throwing the two outside birds first and the center bird last, this is the simplest triple we can ask Pup to run. Pup will instinctively take out the middle bird first, and that will leave the two outside birds separated by a large distance and angle. This makes their appearance clear in Pup's vision, with no clutter in his peripheral vision.

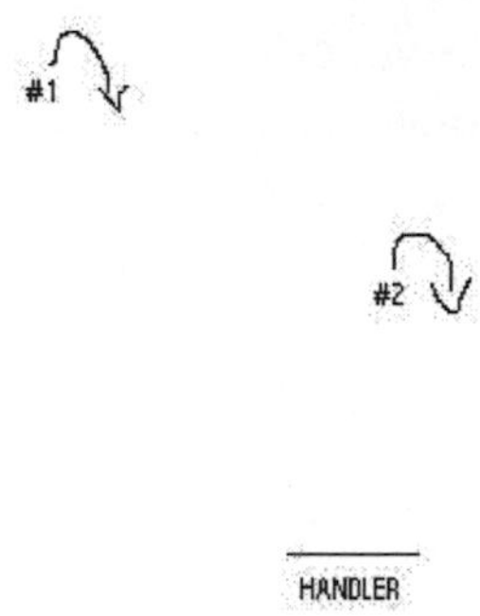

We will go back to doubles for a little while to look at a few more marking concepts. One of the most popular concepts seen in the event world is called a "hip pocket" and is shown in the above diagram. The bird stations are located at different distances from each other, but at close angles. Both stations throw their birds in the same direction. The memory bird is located between the bird stations. This requires Pup to pick up his first bird outside the stations but, then, run back between the stations for his memory bird. Pup's vision is very cluttered in this scenario, with both bird stations in his view. I have yet to see a dog run this drill successfully without schooling. Most Pups will attempt to run outside the bird stations on one side or the other. Schooling and repetition will give Pup the confidence he needs to complete this puzzle. In the diagram, I like to start hip pocket concepts by having #1 throw his bird to the right, and, then, have #2 throw his bird to the right also. After picking up bird #2, Pup is required to push behind bird station #2 to bird #1. When Pup masters this routine, I change the order and direction of delivery. Bird #2 comes out first, going to the left, followed by bird #1, going to the left. Now, Pup must remember the angle and the shorter distance. Unless you are running in very short cover, expect to repeat this drill a few times before Pup figures it out.

Our next concept is called a “flower pot”, shown below, because, when the marks come out of the station, they resemble flowers in a pot. Both marks are thrown from the same station, but in opposite directions. Pup learned this skill in our marking pattern, but, now, he must run this as multiple marks instead of as singles. Pup will have a tendency to go back to his first mark and hunt an old fall, because these marks are so close together. Bird throwers with strong arms help the introduction by creating more distance between the two falls. Gradually, the throws can be shortened to tighten the angle and add difficulty, as Pup’s abilities grow.

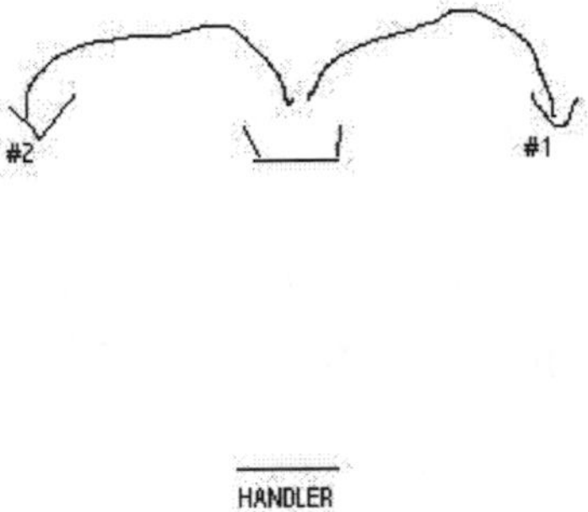

Another concept that we addressed in our marking pattern is the “over and under.” Both of these marks are directly in line with each other and require that Pup precisely define falls of different depths. After picking up bird #2, most Pups will want to stop and hunt the same area (#2) on their way out to #1. As with all of our marking, separating these two marks will make them much easier in your initial work. As Pup learns to focus on his distances, you can tighten the distances between #1 and #2. As with the “hip pocket”, I have never seen a dog successfully run this scenario on his first exposure without schooling.

#3 #2

#1

HANDLER

Going back to triples, a trick that judges love to play on Pup’s eyes involves an “inverted” memory bird. In the above presentation, the memory bird is shorter and usually between the first two birds that are retrieved. Pup must remain focused and have an excellent handle on depth perception if he is to be successful here. You can help Pup with this presentation by placing bird #1 in open cover, so he can find it without having to exert a lot of effort initially. If Pup struggles with this concept, I may school bird #1 several times before running the complete triple. This will prevent Pup from following his instincts and wanting to push deep.

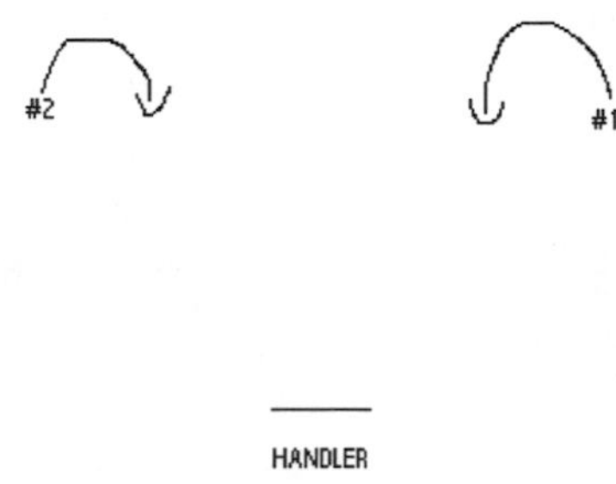

The final concept occurs when two bird stations throw their birds at each other. This is termed “converging marks”, as each mark converges on the other. Pup must run between both bird stations for each retrieve. This is a very cluttered picture in Pup’s view, with two bird stations and two birds all in the same angle. Depending upon the distance between the marks, this can be very simple or almost impossible. Start schooling converging marks with a lot of separation, and move the marks closer as Pup’s abilities allow.

In all of these scenarios, incorporate as many hazards (decoys, terrain, cover, hay bales, etc.) as possible. Pup must learn to maintain his focus in the face of these distractions, until he gets to the point that they offer no incentive. Be careful not to add too many distractions with very tight angles and long distances at the same time.

Conquer the distance and angles before bringing on the hazards.

After completing the above situations on land, it is time to head back to our ponds and make sure Pup can perform the same skills in the water that he does on land. In our earlier drills, Pup learned to go straight and avoid falling into the traps that tempt him. Continue this idea by having Pup run the marking concepts in the water, down banks, across points, and by points. As Pup progresses, both you and the bird throwers back away from the water's edge, and ask Pup to take varying angle entries and exits on his retrieves. Use the skills mastered in earlier sessions to show Pup what you expect.

Before I go any further let me stress something. We have laid out a program that requires time and consistency. This chapter is not something Pup will master in a week or two. It may take six months to a year to cover all the ideas we have addressed. I do not run multiple marked retrieves more often than one day each week with our dogs. The other training days, we run the same concepts discussed in this chapter as singles. By this, Pup gradually masters the ideas in a comfortable fashion. I know trainers who never run multiple marks after their dogs learn how to put triples together. The interesting thing is that my dogs and their dogs perform nicely when asked to run cold (unschooled) multiples. Single marks build confidence in Pup, and his confidence in himself determines how well he performs on marked retrieves. All of Pup's marking problems can be corrected by going back to simple single marked retrieves. Don't be afraid or ashamed to go back there, if needed.

FINISHED DOG

We have talked about what Pup sees and how to school him, but what do we do when things do not go as planned? There is a multitude of problems that can occur when we put more than one mark down at a time for Pup. Switching, or running from one area of a fall to another, is probably the most common problem that you will have to deal with. Many trainers blow a fuse when their dogs switch. Don't go there— keep your cool, and let Pup work out his problems.

Usually, a dog will pick up one bird, and, as he is on the way to another, remember where he was successful with his last retrieve. Pup may decide to run back to the area where he picked up an earlier bird and hunt again. There are plenty of ideas on how to correct this problem and most of them revolve around physical pressure. I have done most of them at some point in my career and was never satisfied with the results. So, I began to allow Pup to return to the old fall and hunt until his heart was content. There was nothing there for him, so he could never gain his reward. After a while, most dogs figure out the error of their ways and proceed over to the proper bird. In doing this, they accepted failure on their own terms and worked out the problem themselves. This dog may think about going back to an old fall at some time, but he also realizes there is no reward for him there. Most importantly, he figured out how to recover from the situation on his own, and I think you know how I feel about that. He accepted it, instead of us forcing it on him.

There are some dogs that cannot figure out the problem and stay in the area of an old fall. Have your bird thrower help Pup find the proper mark if this should happen to you. Immediately, repeat the marks again until Pup gets it right. And then, there is the dog that has this fault as a consistent problem every week in training. For the non e-collar dog, let him go to the old fall area and hunt. While he is in that area, stop him with your whistle and verbally accost him with a heavy "No." Then, have your helper call Pup over to the proper mark.

For the e-collar trainer the correction is very similar. As Pup is hunting in the incorrect area, stop him with your whistle, *nick* with your e-collar and have your helper call Pup to the correct area for his reward. This may take time to correct the problem for the headstrong Pup so, be patient. Your safety net is always in the form of your helper. He can make Pup successful at any time you choose. This is why I do not recommend the use of a mechanical launcher when training on marked retrieves. If Pup gets into trouble, there is little way to correct his mistakes. I can hear some of you now saying that the problem is easy to correct by handling Pup over to the correct mark. Please do not do this.

Handling on marks is a very bad thing, in my opinion. Each time you blow your whistle to stop Pup, you are taking some of Pup's confidence away from him. Remember, his ability to mark is related to how much confidence he has in himself. Before you decide to handle Pup on a mark, ask yourself why is he having this problem? Is Pup not ready for the difficult scenario you presented him? If this is the case, let your helper bail Pup out. If, however, this is a consistent problem, you must decide if Pup is refusing to do what he should or if is he still confused. For the confused Pup, go back to simple marks and make life easy.

For the bold Pup that refuses to perform, emphatically handle him to the bird. This guy is telling you that he is in control on his marks and that he chooses not to pick them up as a way to challenge us. This is a blatant display of displacement behavior that we discussed in the opening chapter. I have seen this a few times, and it has almost always been in a dog that has a lot of confidence. It is not a problem for this dog to find his mark— he simply chooses not to do so. When he displays such actions, run the marks as blind retrieves. Without fail, every dog that displayed such behavior with me gave it up when he realized that I would make decisions for him. Look for the swallows— he will tell you what is on his mind.

Another problem that Pups display on marked retrieves is hunting short of the area where the bird is located. Most Pups have a distance fixation that was conditioned by their trainer. When Pup reaches the conditioned distance, he stops and begins to hunt. Any mark further than this distance will involve a prolonged hunt. You need to retrain Pup's eyes by gradually throwing longer marks in sparse cover.

The opposite problem occurs when Pup decides to hunt past the mark. Most trainers call this hunting deep. This dog may have a vision problem that is demonstrated by his lack of depth perception. You can help his eyesight improve by continually varying the distance of your retrieves and running in open cover. He will be successful, due to the lack of cover, and, as this occurs, he will become more confident in his vision.

A common problem that happens when you run Pup in heavy cover is for him to pass through the area that holds the bird. He did not smell the bird and prefers to search open areas, rather than in the heavy cover. The path of least resistance causes him to fail again. Seeding the area with multiple birds can help Pup when he gets into the area. He needs to develop more focus, and stirring his nose is a step in the right direction. Repeat the scenario until Pup gets it right.

We mentioned the Pup that runs around on his marks earlier, but I will address this again. I have seen dogs run out to their marks and hunt everywhere but the location of the bird. They know exactly where the bird is, but refuse to go to that area as a way to refuse our command to retrieve. In almost every case, these dogs are feeling pressure somewhere else in training. They choose to display their feelings on marked retrieves. By now, Pup has learned that he is in control on marked retrieves, so he challenges us in this portion of his work. For the occasional sinner, I turn my head and let Pup exhaust himself in a prolonged hunt. The repeat offender is not treated so nicely. I will handle him with sharp and demonstrative casts in an effort to jumpstart Pup's focus.

Some Pups will choose to issue the same challenge at the line before we send them to retrieve. They choose not to look at the mark, in spite of our helper's best rendition of a mallard, by turning their head and refusing to look at the bird. In Pup's mind, if I do not look at it, then maybe I will not have to go retrieve it (displacement behavior, once again). Pup's avoidance can be corrected by shortening the marks to a distance where he cannot refuse to see the marks. This problem has resolved itself in short order when Pup realizes that he has to go when commanded.

Head swinging can also occur when trainers throw too many multiple marks. Pup does not want to focus on his last mark, because he is expecting another, more enticing mark to appear. This can progress to a point where Pup will turn his head away from a bird while it is still in the air in anticipation of his next mark. The first time you see this with Pup, do not run anything but single marked retrieves for a week or two. I have seen some trainers allow this problem to grow to a point where Pup was searching for marks instead of watching them down. Pup had little or no idea where the birds were located. He was satisfying his need to chase, but not focusing.

The most worrisome problem I see from Pup is when he smells the roses on his way out to the bird. Pup is ambling around, sniffing and looking at anything that catches his eye. This is the result of a lack of focus and/or desire in the dog. In other words, Pup is poorly bred and has no desire to work. There is little motivation for him. If your dog is doing this, do yourself and him a favor by purchasing another Pup. It can be very frustrating for the two of you if his heart is not in it.

As we stated before, Pup's ability to perform nice marked retrieves depends on how much self-confidence he has. Any time Pup shows a problem on marks, we can make life easier by having our helper assist him, shortening marks and locating them in light cover. Schooling him on difficult concepts will make the transition easier, so send him to school on all of his multiple marked retrieves. Also, spend the majority of your training time on singles. Pup will show how much he likes this in his focus and attitude.

FINISHED DOG

CHAPTER THIRTY-EIGHT

How can Pup learn to honor another dog's work and be happy?

Whether you plan on training a National Field Champion or just a plain old hunting dog, Pup must learn how to comfortably sit and watch as another dog retrieves. We call this honoring. A hunting dog will constantly be asked to honor another Pup, whether in the duck marsh, dove field, goose pit or pheasant drive. My favorite movie is *Lonesome* Dove, and in that flick, Captain Woodrow Call has a line that fits exactly what we are describing. Captain Call said, "I hate rude behavior in man. I won't tolerate it." I feel the same way about my dogs as Woodrow felt about men. Failure to honor another dog's work is simply rude behavior and should never be tolerated. But, how do we get Pup to be a good citizen and happily watch another dog retrieve his birds?

This is done in an honor drill. It requires another somewhat finished dog as a working partner. He will be designated as the working dog and must be trustworthy enough not to interfere with our honor student. We will have the working dog make retrieves in front the honor dog, with the two dogs separated by some distance initially. Keep the honor dog on an EZ-lead to control Pup until you can evaluate how ready he is to accept this situation.

The setup needs to be very controlled, so neither dog is allowed to get into trouble. A helper is a must in this drill, as no retrieves are to be made unless the dogs mind their manners by remaining motionless until sent for the retrieve. Should either dog break to retrieve before being sent, your helper must pick the bumper up before the dog gets to the area.

With everyone in place, begin by having your helper blow his duck call and throw a bumper visible to both dogs. After both dogs are comfortable and under control, the working dog should be sent to retrieve. If the honor dog moves, correct him with a sharp tug on the leash and verbal, *No-Sit!* If you have an e-collar dog, correct him with *Sit-nick-Sit.* Repeat the scenario until our honor student sits perfectly still, without any challenge.

As Pup accepts this scenario, remove the lead and continue to repeat the routine. Gradually, move the dogs closer to each other, as Pup's abilities allow. Make sure the working dog does not learn any bad habits by breaking before being sent. Move your helper in so that the bumpers are now falling directly in front of both dogs. Later, move the dogs closer and closer until they are seated directly beside each other. Any failures by the honor dog must be corrected in a way that he has been conditioned to accept.

We need to entice Pup a little more, and we will do this by having our helper throw a dead bird instead of a bumper. Pup is still at our side, so correcting him should be easy if he decides to move. After both dogs are working well together, switch from a dead bird to a shackled duck. This should motivate Pup to move if he has any inclination to display any rude behavior. From a shackled bird, we will proceed to a shot flyer. Keep a close eye on Pup while going through the routine. Watch for his acceptance as Pup swallows. Be especially careful, should Pup start to avoid the marks by turning his head when they are thrown. Toss him a fun bumper after the drill to reward him for his good behavior.

Most people would be happy with where Pup is now, but let's go to another level. Next, we will do a walk up with both dogs at heel as we walk toward our helper. While we are still walking, the helper will blow his duck call and shoot a flyer in front of the dogs. Command Pup to sit, and have the working handler release his dog to retrieve when the dogs are comfortably under control. Tell Pup what a good dog he is for sitting patiently by your side.

When Pup can handle this, we will now separate ourselves from the dogs as they are seated beside each other. Our helper will toss a bird in front of them for the working dog to retrieve, after both dogs mind their manners. Be prepared to hustle out after Pup if he should try to move for the bird. Some people are happy as long as Pup does not go for the retrieve. Do not tolerate any movement on his part. If he shifts his position or scoots forward even a little, correct him immediately. Our honor student must remain motionless, or we will repeat the drill until he accepts the fact that he cannot move around when placed in this situation.

Later, after Pup has mastered his upland skills, we will quarter the dogs out together. A bird will be launched and shot in front of them. This is the ultimate in an honor. Any dog that can honor another dog's work on a flushed bird while moving away from the handler understands what we are expecting.

This entire process may take a few days or a couple of weeks. Be especially attentive of Pup's attitude during this drill. You can overdo the honor drill and turn Pup off. By asking him to repeatedly honor, we are telling him not to retrieve. This can be taken to a point where Pup will no go. Overcome this temptation by tossing a few fun bumpers as a reward to Pup for doing his job. If his tail is wagging, things are good.

I want to go over the correction process one more time. For the non e-collar dog that moves or attempts to retrieve, correct him with *No-Sit!* on the first offense. On his second error, use *No*- EZ-lead pressure-*Sit* until Pup sits. For the e-collar dog, use *Sit(tweet)-nick-Sit(tweet).* Let his true punishment be that he may never retrieve if he moves. After Pup has the idea, let him retrieve every once in a while to reward him for doing his job. That is a good opportunity for the other dog to do a little honoring.

It is nice for both dogs to have a good relationship with each other. Avoid running this drill with dogs that are not familiar with each other. I like to run this drill with my hunting partner's dog at one of our duck blinds. These Pups are good friends, and this is a very important skill we need them to perform while at this location. We kill two birds with one stone. Think about Captain Call and never tolerate rude behavior in your Pup or anyone else's dog that hunts with you. This is one of the measures of a finished dog and a true pleasure to hunt with.

FINISHED DOG

CHAPTER THIRTY-NINE

Should Pup learn to follow his nose?

Ron Samuels is a good friend of mine from Jetersville, Virginia, and we run into each other at many retriever events. He owns a nice yellow Lab named Gunner who has a very good track record. Ron prides himself on how well Gunner can follow the scent of a bird used in trailing tests. At an event in Georgia, I passed Ron on the road as he was leaving for the long drive back to Virginia. When I asked how Gunner had performed on the trail, Ron said, "He killed it." I laughed so hard that I almost hit a tree with my truck.

When we think of a dog killing a test, it usually revolves around the animal stepping on all three marks in a triple or lining a difficult blind. But Ronnie was serious about how Gunner had performed on the trailing test. He takes a great deal of time when training his dogs to follow a trail. Trailing is one of the main skills a dog can perform that we cannot. He can smell the scent left by a bird making him extremely valuable when a crippled bird hot foots away from us. I can think of numerous times when I have seen dogs demonstrate how strong this scent is to their noses and how instinctive it is for them to follow that scent.

So, how do we train Pup to follow his nose? Just as with all other training, we want Pup to learn the drill first, and then condition that response by repeating the drill until the skill is mastered. Many dogs learn to trail, but their owners fail to condition the response due to a lack of repetition. They see Pup follow the bird and successfully return with the bird a couple of times. A couple of times does not justify a conditioned response.

For a dog to learn how to follow the scent left by a bird, we must maintain as much control over the training process as possible. Control of the dog will be accomplished by a placing Pup on a leash and leading him down the first few trails. A freshly killed duck or pheasant will give us a scent trail that we can drag where we desire.

There is considerable debate over training Pup to trail and when to begin the process. I am a strong believer in starting as soon as Pup has mastered his obedience and force fetch programs. Then, you can control Pup's actions with obedience commands and ensure his picking up the bird with a properly conditioned force fetch. The most important point is to give trailing a separate command and only use that command when Pup is following a scent trail. You can use whatever word or words you wish but I like *Find It*, because it sounds like no other command we will use.

To begin the actual training scenario, kill a duck or pheasant in the spot you wish for the trail to originate. Pull out a handful of feathers from the underside of the bird, and place them at the start of the trail. Tie a rope to the bird and drag it in a straight line, preferably into the wind for about twenty-yards. Untie the bird and leave it at the end of the trail. Go get Pup and put him on a leash. Walk him at heel to the feather pile and command him to *Sit*. Hopefully, Pup will be excited with the smell of a bird in his nose, but if he is not, stir the feathers for him to see and smell. Now it is time for him to begin working the trail. Walk Pup at heel down the trail while commanding *Find It* every few feet until he is at the end of the trail picking up the bird. If he balks at the bird, command him to *Fetch*.

On this first trail, we are trying to demonstrate what *Find It* means by restricting Pup's movements so that he cannot leave the scent cone of the trail. This trail should be very easy since we are working into the wind. After a number of repetitions, Pup will begin to scent the trail and follow his nose to the bird on his own. Gradually, we will make the trails more difficult by dragging them with the wind, and, later, across the wind. Then, Pup should know what *Find It* means and understand how to follow his nose. It is time to condition the response.

Conditioning involves repeating the exercise until Pup will perform the desired response in the face of distractions. This can be done at any time during the day. Returning from a hunt with fresh birds is a great opportunity to do a little conditioning. You can work on trailing early in the morning, before going to work, or after supper, in the dark. It requires no helpers or daylight, and it takes only a few minutes to set up and complete the training scenario. Your neighbors may question your sanity when they see you dragging a dead duck around the yard, so be prepared.

What you drag for Pup to follow is important at first. I like to start with freshly killed birds, but, as his proficiency grows, I may drag thawed birds from the freezer, frozen birds, or even plastic training bumpers. It will amaze you how quickly Pup can focus on even the smallest amount of scent and follow the trail for his reward at the end. Later, when he has mastered his skills, we will turn loose a wing-clipped bird and let the fun begin. Pup's tail will wag a little quicker, and his concentration will be a lot stronger.

This brings us to another point that is constantly debated. Some dogs will follow the trails with their heads down and noses to the ground. Other Pups will go down the trail with their heads straight up in the air. In both scenarios the same thing is happening. They are following scent, but doing it in varying styles. Sadly, I have seen judges at retriever events penalize a dog that trails with his head in the air, even though he went directly to the bird. They felt like Pup did not trail because his nose was not on the ground. If we knew what Pup smelled, and how he followed scent, it would be easier to criticize. But, for all we know the dog with his nose in the air may have superior trailing abilities because he does not need to put his face to the ground. Your guess is as good as mine.

Trailing can be one the most impressive skills that a dog possesses. I have seen my old Lab, Hank, trail a running pheasant at a NAHRA Invitational for nearly half a mile before returning to heel with a wagging tail and pheasant in his mouth. I have also seen my hunting partner's dog, Boomer, trail a crippled mallard across several hundred yards of water before pulling the bird out of a beaver lodge. The concentration these dogs exhibited was well-conditioned through repetitive training in a program that believes a dog should trail. Both of these animals were also confident markers and ran very precise blinds. Pup can have it all if we separate the commands and take the time to properly train him to follow his nose.

At some time, whether you hunt or run events, Pup will need the ability to follow his nose. You may have a crippled pintail down in the marsh that appeared to be wearing some hardware on its leg. Or, you may be at the NAHRA Invitational only needing to complete the trail to qualify as a member of the All-American team. In both cases, Pup will be comfortable in his performance if you take the time to condition the proper responses. Then you can go around and tell all your hunting buddies that you are like Ron Samuels, because you have a dog that can "kill" a trail.

FINISHED DOG

CHAPTER FORTY

How does Pup learn to become a happy upland hunter?

Quartering or hunting a field in search of scent is a lot like retrieving. It is a natural instinct born into our dogs. Our job as a trainer is to awaken those instincts and control the actions of Pup as he learns until a conditioned response appears. I see this quite often at retriever events where a dog wanders through the field, never out of control but not really sure what he should be doing. These Pups learned how to quarter but the conditioning process was passed over. I am not sure if the trainers were satisfied with these performances, or if they were too busy perfecting their marks and blinds, not having enough time to train on quartering.

Training Pup to quarter can and should begin as soon as you bring your future star home from the breeder. A long daily walk will reap multiple benefits for a young Pup. It presents him with many new smells, sounds, sights and adventures. Pup will want to go exploring, but it is unlikely that he will range too far from you. As Pup is bounding around in front of you, start communicating to him that you like his actions with a happy *Hunt'em Up.*

So, Pup is running through the fields as happy as if he had two tails. Initially, your job is to follow him in whatever direction he goes. Pup must learn that his place is in front of you. If he decides to run behind you, turn and follow him so that he is always in front of you. I have seen older dogs really struggle with this concept. They thought the safe place for them was at heel. More than one field trial washout has come to me for upland training with little or no understanding of upland skills. These Pups were well conditioned and secure in the heel position. With patience, they all came around to become good upland hunters. As young dogs, their hunting instinct was never nurtured. Avoid this by starting early, and incorporate a daily walk into a training routine on quartering. Pup will have a blast and never realize that he is being trained, so don't tell him.

As Pups grow older, they tend to become a little more independent and may decide to challenge you. On one of your daily walks with Pup, he will decide to venture off on his own. Pup is bold now and ready to challenge your authority, so be prepared when this happens. Hopefully, you have already started some obedience training, and Pup understands the *Here* command. It is time to start incorporating some obedience into the quartering process. Use the *Here* command to call Pup back toward you each time he ventures too far from you. With enough repetition, Pup will learn how far he is allowed to stray while hunting. This distance is determined by how well you shoot and what type of birds you are hunting.

I would also encourage you to use your whistle at this time. If you already have Pup obeying the whistle, it will be easy for him to learn your gun range. Give a *tweet-tweet* on the whistle each time he ventures out too far, and, before you know it, Pup will be turning on his own when he reaches that distance from you. Now, we are getting somewhere— Pup is happy while hunting, but under control.

I am a big believer in buying the best Pup you can and letting his natural genetic encoding tell him where to hunt. However, there are times when we need to cast Pup into a specific area, because we feel like there may be birds in that area, or maybe we actually saw them there. To do this, Pup must learn hand signals. Unlike blind retrieves, casting in the upland hunt is not a precise exercise, but a steering of Pup into a general area.

A dog will easily learn to cast in an upland hunt if he will come when called. Start off by commanding Pup to *Hunt'em up.* When he goes out in one direction, you veer off in the other. As he is about to turn on his own, give a *tweet-tweet* on the whistle, causing him to turn and come toward you. When Pup looks up at you, hold out your arm pointing in the direction you are heading. Start walking a zig-zag pattern through the field on your daily treks. If Pup zigs, you zag and if he zags, you zig. Each time he turns, either on his own or after you call him, hold out the correct arm and cast him in a new direction. With enough repetition and conditioning, Pup will easily cast in any direction you need.

One of the reasons Pup needs to learn casting is to be able to put his nose in a particular piece of cover that we believe holds birds. But, what if our Pup decides he would rather run around the cover instead of punching into it and hunting? We need to show him that the cover is a good place and not something of which to be afraid. Do this by walking into the cover yourself and call him in there with you. If he likes you and will come when called, this should not be too difficult. After he enters the cover encourage him to hunt with *Hunt'em up* in an upbeat tone. When Pup finds enough birds in the cover, you will have a hard time keeping him out of there.

So far, we have presented an idealistic picture, with Pup obeying our commands and hunting freely when commanded *Hunt'em up.* But, what if he shows little interest in the field and is lethargic in his hunt? Try spicing up the field with a few birds, either freshly killed or live flyers. Hopefully, this will jolt Pup's interest to warp speed and excite him. Spread the birds out on both sides of the field to encourage Pup to hunt the sides. Walk down the middle while Pup hunts the sides and retrieves the planted birds. Make a big fuss over him each time he finds a bird, and then cast him off to hunt again with *Hunt'em up.*

I hunt varying types of cover and try to introduce Pup to all within my reach. Grouse reside in wooded thickets on steep hillsides. Quail in our area stay on the fringes of soybean fields, and the Midwest pheasants can range from chest high CRP to flooded cattails. Figure out what you want your dog to hunt, and put him in that type of cover as often as you can. Variety is the spice of life, according to one of my divorced friends, so spice up Pup's life with a little variety in cover and terrain.

Quartering can be a great joy in your dog's life, if it is properly presented. Many trainers use this as a way to relieve pressure on Pup when things get tough, much like a fun bumper. Start early and take your time, as Pup learns to hunt. Repeat this scenario on a regular basis with Pup until he displays the conditioned responses you need. Then stand back and watch his tail wag— it will be hard to tell which one of your is happier.

FINISHED DOG

CHAPTER FORTY-ONE

Do you want Pup to be steady to wing, shot and fall when upland hunting?

I am very fortunate that I get to travel to the Midwest each fall. On this trip, friends and I pursue wild pheasants, quail and prairie chickens. There are many pleasures that unfold on our annual pilgrimage. First, is the camaraderie of old friends getting together in the outdoors away from telephones and business constraints. Next, and most important to me, is watching a group of talented and well-trained dogs work the fields.

Usually early on opening morning, one of these finely tuned machines we call dogs gets more than a little excited and decides to chase a flushed bird. The whistle blowing begins as the owner's face reddens. He is blushing, partly from forcing as much air as possible through his whistle, but mostly from the embarrassment of his Master Hunter not performing in a masterly fashion.

It is not long before the debate over training a dog to become steady begins. Some of the guys suggest that a breaking dog will get to the downed bird quicker and decrease the chances of losing a crippled rooster. Being a trainer, my hackles go up each time I hear this. The debate carries on over the course of the morning's hunt, and a bird or three is spared the table, because we are discussing training techniques instead of focusing on swinging the muzzle of a shotgun past a ringneck's head.

FINISHED DOG

Having a dog steady when a bird flushes is important to me for several reasons. First and foremost is safety for Pup. If the flushing bird is a low flyer and Pup is in hot pursuit, even the best shooting eye can put some lead shot in Pup's hide. Each year I receive a story of someone's dog that was either blistered or killed from this lack of control.

Another reason Pup should steady is related to my job as a professional trainer. My daily goal is to produce a finished dog that remains under control and obeys his handler in the face of all distractions. Allowing Pup to chase a flushed bird is letting him do as he pleases, and this becomes very self-serving for him. Pup is assuming the alpha role in this scenario.

The last topic to discuss on the theory of remaining steady is strictly for the hunter. If we are pheasant hunting and a hen flushes, Pup needs to sit still without chasing that bird across the field. Should Pup pursue the hen, he is likely to flush more birds out of gun range. A dog that does this repeatedly will most likely have an owner that gets to hunt by himself. His hunting partners will soon find someone else to spend their fall afternoons with.

So, we are resolved to train Pup to remain steady when a bird rises from under his nose. How does he learn this skill? There are a few prerequisites before you can begin. Pup must be very obedient, not only at heel, but at any distance from you. While being conditioned to stop on a whistle blast helps, it is not mandatory. He must also know how to enthusiastically quarter a field in search of birds. Lastly, you are going to need some help. A friend or hunting partner should handle the birds while you control Pup. If you cannot find a helper, a mechanical bird launcher will do. There are many types available, from simple boxes to elaborate radio-controlled devices.

The approach to steadiness is stepwise, and each step should be mastered before you move on to the next one. Have your helper go into the field with a bird and hide or place the bird-loaded launcher in the field. I use pigeons in my initial training, because they are readily available and inexpensive. Quarter Pup on a long leash toward your helper and, as he becomes excited by the bird's smell, command him to *Sit.* If you have been using a whistle as a way to command Pup to sit, make sure you use it in this drill. If you have never used a whistle, this might be a good time to start.

After Pup is sitting, release the bird with your device or have your helper toss the bird into the air. Continue to command *Sit*, and, if Pup should attempt to get up or chase the pigeon, use your leash to control his actions by making him sit. Repeat this drill until Pup will remain seated when the bird is released. This may take a day or a week, depending on Pup's attitude.

When Pup has mastered this skill, we will continue the same routine, but change the timing of our *Sit* command. Now, have your helper release the pigeon as soon as Pup scents the bird. As the bird flushes, blow your whistle or verbally command *Sit*. Pup should be comfortable with this. If he decides to forget his manners, remind him with a tug on the leash while commanding *Sit* or blowing your whistle. Repeat this until Pup will sit on his own without you having to blow your whistle or command *Sit.*

The next step is to repeat the above drill without your leash being attached to Pup. Be sure that he has mastered the above steps before removing his leash. Some Pups learn to be controllable only while the leash is attached, so keep it handy in case he needs to be corrected. When you can quarter Pup into your bird release or helper and have him sit on his own as the flush occurs, he understands. Repeat this on a regular basis to keep the conditioned response in place.

There are a few things that can happen if you repeat these drills too often. Pup may decide to rush across the field, looking for your helper, so he can get his flush instead of hunting the field. If this happens, do not ignore it or allow Pup to have the flush. That will only enhance the problem. A bird launcher will be of great value here. Move it around the field by never placing it in the same location twice. This will force Pup to hunt for the scent of our birds instead of look for a person.

Another reaction that can occur due to over conditioning is where a dog finds the scent and sits down, waiting for the flush. I have seen this many times at events and a few times in training. Pup is telling you that he knows he cannot chase, so he will go ahead and sit. If this happens, command him to *Hunt'em up* until he moves ahead and flushes the bird. Stroke him on the shoulder and let him know that flushing the bird is what you want. Later, we will reward him with a shot bird.

Now that Pup has learned to be steady on a flushed bird, how does he learn to remain seated for the shot and fall? Before we approach this in the upland field, Pup must be steady for shot flyers, when training on marked retrieves. After we are sure he is steady at our side, Pup can learn to remain seated while he is many yards ahead of us with hot scent, flapping wings and gunfire over his head. As before, we need a friend to release and shoot the birds while we control Pup's actions.

Have your helper go into the field with birds and a gun. He needs to be coordinated enough to throw a bird and shoot it at the same time. If this is a problem, find more help or use a mechanical launcher to release the bird for him. Hide your helper and equipment in some cover upwind from where you intend to approach the cover.

Start with Pup on your long leash by quartering into the wind toward your helper and the birds. Avoid conditioning bad habits into Pup by rushing out to the flush. Make sure he hunts the field in a proper fashion. As Pup starts to become excited by the bird scent, have your helper release the bird in front of Pup. If he mastered the skill of sitting on the flush, his bottom should be parked on the terra firma. However, if he fails to immediately sit, blow your whistle and/or command *SIT!* in a heavy tone. Then go back and repeat the process until he does sit. Only after Pup is sitting, have your helper shoot the bird. Make this point very clear to your assistant: if Pup does not sit, then he is not to shoot.

Let's say everything went right. Pup sat down without a whistle from you, and your helper shot the pigeon clearly in Pup's view. After the bird hits the ground, command Pup to *Sit* and reinforce that command with a sharp whistle blast. If needed, a tug on the leash will remind him that you are in control and he cannot retrieve until released by you. When you are sure that he is steady and not pulling on the leash, we have a big decision to make. Do we allow Pup to retrieve this bird or do we pick it up while he watches?

I write a great deal about debate over training methods. One of the wonderful traits of canines is that they accept training in whatever form it is presented. Some trainers will encourage their Pup to pick up this bird as a reward for good behavior. Others will reinforce the idea of steadiness by having Pup remain seated while they go pick up the pigeon. What is the best method?

Usually, I let a young dog have his retrieve after he does his job properly. Later, as he demonstrates that he understands the routine, I rarely permit him to retrieve a flushed bird in the training environment. Pup will get his fill of retrieves when we are hunting and will be much less likely to break for the retrieve until sent. When preparing for upland tests, I never allow the dogs to retrieve any of the birds. After the bird hits the ground, and I am are sure Pup is steady, I command him to *Heel.* After he assumes the proper heel position, I walk out and pick the bird up while he watches. In this scenario, Pup learns to remain totally under control and breaking for a shot bird will be a rare occurrence. If you want to reward him for a job well done, toss a fun bumper for Pup off to the side away from the area of the shot bird.

Pup has learned what you want. The next step is conditioning the desired response. Repeat the above scenario, as your helper moves to different locations in different fields. If you do decide to let Pup retrieve any of the downed birds, vary the time between when the bird hits the ground and when you release him to retrieve. Avoid sending him as soon as the bird hits the ground, because this will encourage Pup to break after only a few repetitions. Have Pup remain seated for a few seconds one time and an extended time on the next retrieve. In doing this, he will learn to see you as alpha and leader of the pack.

As Pup becomes trustworthy, remove the leash and allow him to hunt freely through the fields. Keep the leash handy, in case he forgets what a wonderful trainer you are. If errors occur, hook him back up to the leash and repeat the process showing Pup what you desire. Continue the repetitions until you are confident that Pup has mastered his skills. Then, give yourself a pat on the back and Pup a stroke on the shoulder until he says that he understands. You now have a finished upland retriever that is ready for any bird in all types of terrain.

CHAPTER FORTY-TWO

How do you take Pup hunting for the first season?

I was in Charleston, South Carolina last June, conducting a training seminar for a new club. One of the attendees had a nice looking eight-week old chocolate Lab pup, and the owner was quite proud of him. During the day, as we were talking, the owner commented to me that he was planning on taking this Pup hunting on the opening day of dove season, September 1st. I frowned and asked him if he was sure he wanted to take a twenty-week old Pup into a hot dove field for his first hunting experience. The owner insisted this would be good training for his Pup. All I could think of was how confused this dog would surely become with other dogs, loud hunters, continuous shooting, multiple falls, tons of scent and stifling heat. This is not my idea of a nice introduction to hunting.

Before you head to the marsh or field for Pup's virgin hunt, make sure both of you are ready for what is about to happen. If Pup is ready, take him. If he is not, let him watch from the truck. I know many people that have allowed totally unacceptable bad habits to form while hunting, because they were more interested in shooting than in what Pup was doing or thinking. A lot of outstanding training can evaporate in one hunting trip if Pup is allowed to make decisions for himself and not follow your lead. Much of our training is contrary to what Pup's instincts tell him to do. His instinctive tendencies will be greatly exaggerated on this first hunt, so make sure you pay attention to Pup's actions.

For the above reasons, I instruct my clients to either going hunting or training when they take their dogs hunting during Pup's first season. If you want to hunt, leave Pup behind until your need to shoot is satisfied. Then, take Pup out and give him some work. If you choose to train, let someone else shoot the birds while you control Pup. Do not attempt to do both until Pup is comfortable with the situation and has some positive experiences in the field. Initially, I instruct my friends to only shoot singles for my young dogs. After he settles in, stretch Pup out and test the skills that have been conditioned in your training program. Don't be afraid to run doubles, triples, blinds, or honors, as long as Pup has mastered those skills in training and has become comfortable with his surroundings during the hunt.

Each time I discuss the topic of Pup's first hunt, I have flashbacks of my first hunting trip to Nebraska. Hank, my old Lab, was on his first upland hunt, and I was very concerned that he would learn bad habits in this new venue. On this trip, my shooting was much more miserable than normal. At the end of the trip, everyone realized that I had not killed a single bird. As I looked back at what was going on, my attention was so focused on Hank and his actions that I was not keeping my head on the gunstock. In hindsight, this was a very good thing. Hank did not learn any bad upland habits and went on to be one of the best pheasant dogs I have had the pleasure to hunt behind.

There are many problems that can arise during your first hunting trip with Pup. The most common is breaking. You are trying your best to hit a bird while it is darting above you and not paying much attention to Pup. He realizes that you are not focused on him and takes off after a bird on his own, when you are lucky enough to knock one down. With a few successful breaks, Pup will quickly learn that he does not have to remain steady while hunting. Once Pup has been steadied, any breaks must be quickly and firmly dealt with in a fashion that he has conditioned to accept. Most importantly, Pup must not be allowed to retrieve the bird. Do whatever it takes to keep him from picking up his reward.

In a busy dove hunt, I see untrained dogs switch from one downed bird to another without ever completing a retrieve. Pup is in a feeding frenzy with birds rapidly falling around him. Before he can complete one retrieve, he switches to another bird. In this scenario, virtually all of your training is quickly disappearing. That is why I recommend shooting singles only during Pup's first hunt.

Make sure each bird is delivered to hand before another one is shot.

Many dogs have been properly introduced to the gun in training, but become gun shy during a hunt. This is normally the result of someone in the hunting party accidentally blasting Pup's ears. They are paying attention to birds instead of where Pup is sitting. Goose pits and duck blinds are notorious places for this to happen, so be especially careful of Pup's location if you shoot in these places.

You hear me mention dove hunting a great deal, because that is our first opening day each fall. Doves are small birds with lots of tiny feathers that come out with the least contact. Most dogs that have not retrieved these gray rockets will spit them out in an attempt to get the feathers out of their mouths. I have also seen this happen with pheasants, woodcock, grouse and pigeons. Sloppy bird handling is often permitted while hunting, so the hunter can hurry along for the next bird. This can become a lifelong problem if it is not corrected immediately. Pup learned how to properly handle birds during force fetching. Remind him if should become too sloppy with your birds.

There are many other problems with Pup that can interrupt a good day's hunt. The list is almost endless, but the solution to each mistake lies in your drill work. Pup learned how to communicate with you as you learned the language Canuus. Use the skills he has mastered to gain the correct action from Pup in the hunting arena. The most important thing I can say about taking Pup hunting is for you to maintain the exact same standard with him while hunting as you do when training. Even in the face of all the distractions, keep Pup working at the comfortable level you conditioned while training. Should he display problems while hunting, identify them and spend your next training sessions addressing those mistakes with the proper drills to correct his behavior. Hunting is a venue that will test Pup to the utmost. Use your trips into the field as testing ground for your abilities as a trainer. With enough focus and preparation, Pup will measure up on the finished dog measuring stick like Mary Poppins, "practically perfect in every way."

CHAPTER FORTY-THREE

Are there any more skills Pup needs to become an event dog?

Nope, that's all there is.

I cannot tell you how many times a client has come to me stating, "I just want a hunting dog." A year later they are traveling every weekend from event to event, chasing points in hopes of earning titles on their Pup. Training dogs is a great gig, but it becomes more addictive than any drug I ever sold when I was a pharmacist. People start off simply wanting Pup to be obedient. After obedience comes a little retrieving and then blind retrieves. Soon, they own more training equipment than their garage can hold and have to purchase a dog trailer to get their pack of dogs to the events.

There are many venues that will be glad to test your Pup's skills according to their rulebook. The American Kennel

Club offers licensed field trials and hunt tests. The North American Hunting Retriever Association, United Kennel Club and the Canadian Kennel Club all offer hunt tests that will evaluate how proficient Pup is in a hunting environment. There is continual debate over which program is best and who has the best dogs. My statement to that is, they all are good. Each of the programs has a slightly different focus, but they all test the same basic skill— how well can you communicate with your dog, and is he conditioned to perform the challenges of the individual rulebooks?

Should this bug ever bite you, and I am sure it will, sit back and enjoy the ride by not rushing into the race before Pup is ready. Request a rulebook from the testing organization of your choice and be absolutely positive that you understand the rules before going to play. When reading the rulebook, think back on the drills Pup learned. Use the necessary drills Pup has mastered to enhance the skills needed to meet the requirements of the testing organization. In this book, there is a drill that will condition the correct responses for participation in any of the above games.

Pay close attention to the distance requirements in the rulebooks. Make sure Pup is comfortable in his work at those distances. I always train in excess of the rulebook distances, in case my estimate of one hundred yards is short of the judge's view. Both you and Pup will be very frustrated if he is conditioned to work at two hundred yards and the tests are set up at four hundred yards. The point of this is to understand what is expected before you arrive at the event and be confident that Pup is properly prepared.

Regardless of how well prepared you and Pup are, there will be failures. Get used to disappointment, because it is coming if you play the games. On occasion, even the most well prepared dog stumps his toe and fails to perform in his usual standard. Don't get mad at the judges or fellow competitors. Use the events as a way to evaluate your training program and get even with the bad guys by training harder in the areas where Pup had problems. Come back in future weekends, and show the world that you have filled in the holes in Pup's training program by demonstrating with your dog what a finished dog can do.

Events are very good things for current and future dogs. They ensure that the best dogs are used for breeding purposes, by continually putting the successful dogs in front of us. More importantly, the events give you and Pup something to do for the other nine months out of a year when you cannot go hunting together. Pup will form a stronger bond with you because of the extra time spent together. With that stronger bond will come better communication skills in the language Canuus. In turn, the skills will make you and Pup a better hunting team when the season opens again. A huge side effect of events is the number of new friends Pup will introduce you to. I have a hard time imagining my life without the wonderful experiences my dogs have taken me through. We have covered North America from coast to coast and each excursion was a great adventure. If you make it fun and include the family, you will probably be able to talk your spouse into a new truck for your champion to ride in. I only hope you enjoy the rides your Pup takes you as much as I have enjoyed mine.

CHAPTER FORTY-FOUR

How much correction is too much?

Most of this book has dealt with Pup and his take on the world. This one is for you, and it is very important that you understand what I am saying. I have placed this chapter last in the book for a reason— many people skip to the last chapter in a book when reading. It should have been one of the first chapters, but I wanted it to be fresh on your mind, so I put it at the end. It is hard for me to tell you all the things I have seen as a trainer in my years. I watched a dog beaten until the trainer could not stand up any longer, because he was exhausted. I have seen dog's ears that looked like hamburger from excessive force fetching by trainers who did not have a clue what Pup was saying to them. And then, there are the dogs that came to me for training with shot in their hide, broken limbs or missing teeth from excessive force by previous trainers.

As bad as these experiences were, none of them approached the day at my kennel when a dog lost his life at the hands of another trainer. That day changed the way I will forever view how a dog should be trained and treated. It impacted me to the point that I threw away all of my riding crops and vowed no one would ever strike a dog at my kennel again. If you hit a dog around me, expect me to hit you. I began to pay more attention to what a dog said instead of what he did, and my training program has grown greatly by that change. It was a terrible thing to watch a dog die because a trainer lost control of his actions, but maybe some good came out of that day. This event started me on my quest to change how we train dogs and promote the concept of listening to what Pup is saying to you. Open your minds, your eyes and your ears and hear me out.

The status quo says it is okay to hurt a dog when you are training. I say it is not. Many trainers believe they should hurt Pup with physical or electric pressure, if he fails to do as he is told. Abuse is never acceptable in any training program, and there is a very fine line between a professional trainer using a riding crop and abuse. The experienced professional trainer knows how far he can go and keep Pup happy, but the amateur trainer, the person I wrote this book for, has a hard time stopping short of abuse. So, don't go there. When I think back on all the times I used a riding crop or watched another trainer use one, little was learned by the dog taking the licks. The whipping satisfied the trainer's need to get even, but the only thing Pup gleaned from this was to fear a person wielding something in his hand.

Throughout this program, Pup has learned how to be corrected for his misbehavior in a standard that is comfortable for him. Do not be tempted to go outside that standard when you lose your cool. Pup will not understand the change, and you will feel bad about your actions when things settle down. Be consistent in each training session, and if you begin to lose control of your emotions, put Pup up until you can regain your focus.

Avoid training while consuming alcohol. Pup may misread your posture, or you may misread what he is telling you because of the spirits. If you are tired or not feeling good, think about giving Pup the day off. The majority of my bad training days at the kennel are the result of not sleeping well the night before. The dogs see I am not my usual self and take on an entirely different posture in training on those days. If you must train on days when you feel bad, keep the training session simple for Pup. Every Friday at my kennel is called "No Fail Friday", because we make things very straight forward and simple. It is a great way to put the dogs up for the weekend or prepare for an upcoming weekend event. They feel good about their week and look forward to the next training session.

I feel like a recovering alcoholic when I talk about abuse in the training world. At one time, I was probably as bad as anyone out there, because I thought that was how we were supposed to train. There are many times I stepped over the line and made mistakes with too much pressure on dogs. Learn from my mistakes by not doing that to your dog. Let that stay on my ticket with God and off yours.

You have learned how to communicate with Pup. Watch and listen to what he has to say, because he will tell you how he feels about everything around him. Delmar Smith told me a long time ago that Pup will always tell you what has happened to him by his actions, and he will never lie about it. After all my years of training, I could not agree more. Pay attention to what Pup is saying. Understand how to correct him when he is wrong, and reward him when he is right.

Pressure, and Pup's perception of it, is the cause of almost all of the problems I have discussed so far. There are three out responses Pup will try in the face of pressure. His first option will be to bolt away from the cause of his pressure, you. In his mind, if he moves away from pressure, it has less control over him. For a bolting Pup, we have discussed the debolting drill during collar conditioning phase of training. Review this if necessary, but always evaluate what is causing the problem before you attempt to solve the puzzle. Eliminating the problem may make your training, and Pup's life, easier.

In my career, I have been bitten by a few dogs and deserved most of the bites. Pup bites when he is feeling pressure and can no longer bolt away from the pressure. In the bite or attack mode, he attempts to make the pressure go away from him. This creates the same separation from pressure that he perceives to be a problem, just as during a bolt. Pup will probably try to bluff his way out before he bites by showing his teeth or growling. Listen to what he is saying, and find a solution before one of you gets hurt.

If biting does occur, it can lead to unthinkable problems. One of my friends purchased a very expensive, well-bred Puppy and took it to a trainer in South Carolina. He went down to work with the trainer on one particularly hot day. After lunch, they went into the office for a cold drink. My friend's Pup was having a lot of trouble learning how to enter anything. The trainer decided to use a cattle prod as a way to push the Pup into his kennel. With enough prodding, Pup would enter whatever opened in front of him. When the trainer opened the refrigerator door for a cold beverage, Pup jumped into the refrigerator thinking he was supposed to kennel. Try as they might, they could not pry him from the inside of the refrigerator. The trainer decided that he would prod Pup out of the icebox and put the juice to the young dog while he was sitting inside the refrigerator. Pup's back was against the wall, and he saw no way out so he bit the prod. He bit it so hard that the cattle prod snapped in two. Pup learned a very bad lesson that day. In his mind, when pressure presented itself, all he had to do was bite and pressure would go away. My friend's wonderful young dog became untrainable and was shortly put to sleep, because he continued to bite each time he was asked to work. Nobody was listening to that Pup while he was sitting in the refrigerator, and it was likely that the trainer never listened to what any Pup had to say.

If your Pup tries to bite, not Puppy play bite, but "I want to hurt you" bite, identify why he is displaying this action. Did you push him too far into a corner and place Pup in a situation where he has no other options? If that is the case, this is your fault and you need to get the pressure off that dog while apologizing to him. You probably deserve the broken skin and scars left behind.

Occasionally a dog will bite without any provocation. It has happened to me once, and that dog hurt me very badly. Unprovoked bites are scary things, and I have found little solution other than to put these dogs to sleep. As with my friend's Pup, once they learn to bite, it becomes progressively worse. They become a tremendous liability, and you can never turn your back on them.

Pup's last attempt to avoid pressure is by lying down and saying, "I quit." This guy has given up and would rather take any beating than perform. Get him moving as quickly as possible by whatever means in an effort to demonstrate what will ease his pressure. Pup is telling you that he cannot handle his predicament. It is your job to figure out what is the cause and how you can solve the problem.

Any time Pup displays the bolt, bite or quit behavior, you need to change your training session and your communication method. I go to Canuus, speaking his language when things get tough. Pup may not always understand our words, but nothing will ever be lost in translation when you speak his dialects with posture, tone and touch. Make sure you do more than lecture Pup in his language by listening to what he has to say. Often Pup will tell you what is on his mind and that will make your job as a trainer much easier, so listen to him.

The status quo training methods will soon come under much scrutiny. Our animal protectionist friends will change our ways for us if we don't do it ourselves. Stop the abuse that some people call dog training by always looking for a better method to train. Pup will work harder for you and both of you will be happier when you make things easy. Speak to Pup in a language he understands, and always pay attention to what he has to say to you. Canuus is a strong language, and you should now know how to translate it. Keep your conversations positive, and never lie to Pup. If you treat him right, he will never lie to you, and honesty builds eternally strong relationships. Good training and happy hunting.

Hunting Retriever Champion, Grand Master Hunting Retriever CJ'S Shortstop better known as "Scoop" and his sidekick Charlie